Martin Solutions Group
ISBN:

Covered: The 4-Essential Pillars that will Safeguard, Support, and Restore Your Marriage
© 2020 by Kenyon and Taccara Martin
All Rights Reserved

No part of this book may be reproduced, stored in a retrieval system, or transmitted by any means without the written permission of the authors.

Interior Design and Layout by Brittany Mays of BMays.com

Cover Design by Taccara Martin

COVERED

The 4-Essential Pillars That Will Safeguard, Support and Restore Your Marriage

Kenyon & Taccara Martin

Dedication

To our pastors and mentors (in business and relationships), Joel and Patricia Gregory.

You are our earthly example of God's design for covering. You don't profess to be perfect in marriage, but your integrity, devotion, and commitment to growing in love is admirable. Thank you for who you are. And thank you for promoting, protecting, and cultivating a community where Godly marriage is safe and supported.

We pray that this book impacts marriages the way you both have impacted ours.

About the Authors

Leveraging their education in Theology, Psychology, and Christian Counseling, Kenyon and Taccara Martin have designed counseling services, books, and virtual programs to help individuals and couples break toxic relationship habits and learn the habits of healthy love. They have been trained by the Gottman Institute and are MBTI certified and use their knowledge and skill to use research-backed concepts to help people overcome some of their most challenging relationship experiences.

They are the authors of 2 books, Covered for marriages, and Journey to Freedom, The Soul-Ties® Detox, and their resources have been used in singles ministries, small groups, and book clubs to help bring healing to local communities across the nation and abroad.

Together, Kenyon and Taccara have 6 children and 1 grandchild. They reside in Atlanta, Georgia where they attend and serve at LinkedUP church under Pastors Joel and Patricia Gregory.

For booking and other information, visit AskTheMartins.com.

Table of Contents

How to Use This Book .... Pg. 8

For Small Group Leaders .... Pg. 11

About the 4-Pillars .... Pg. 14

Introduction .... Pg. 22

Safety .... Pg. 28

Security .... Pg. 60

Trust .... Pg. 80

Empathy .... Pg. 96

Repairing Broken Pillars .... Pg. 122

How to Use This Book

This book will provide opportunities for sensitive—and sometimes intense—conversations. At each juncture, you and your spouse will be given opportunities to matter to each other in ways that perhaps neither of you have dealt with before. We want you to affirm each other's importance, feelings, and perspective through each conversation. If you want to be successful in this process, you should approach each conversation with care and purpose. Each chapter, and their corresponding questions, has been designed to help you see yourself through the reflection of your spouse. Hearing your spouse's needs is sometimes hard, but if you spend too much time being defensive, you will become deaf to your spouse's needs, and they yours. Repeat this to yourself: "This book is for me."

If you and your spouse are reading through the book together, treat it like your marital "small group" or book club. Schedule time to read each chapter by yourselves, give time and space for reflection and answering questions, and then schedule a separate time to meet so that you can discuss your questions and answers with one another. Husbands, we challenge you to allow your wife to go first. This will give you an opportunity to demonstrate servant leadership by allowing her to be served first. This is not a requirement, but a challenge.

Avoid Censorship

When you are answering the questions from each section, it's important to not censor or hide your feelings. Give yourself (and your spouse) permission to feel with honesty and vulnerability. Avoiding honesty in these moments just to "keep the peace" will defeat the purpose of the exercises and the book as a whole. If you ever feel the need to hide your honest feelings from your spouse, please consider involving a trusted professional (i.e. pastoral counselor, marriage counselor, marriage coach, or mentor). They will help you and your spouse by mediating and navigating the difficult aspects of the conversation to ensure you both are heard. Since you will be exposing your hearts to one another, this entire process will require the utmost trust in each other to be delicate and sensitive with the other's vulnerabilities.

With that understood, it's important not to confuse hostility with vulnerability. Being honest or vulnerable is no excuse for contempt, harsh criticism, or personal attacks. While we want you to be honest and not hide vulnerabilities, it's equally as important to be careful with your responses to one another's vulnerabilities. Always filter your responses through love and respect first by thinking, *How would I want to receive this information if it were being communicated to me?* Even if you are not entirely "skilled" at using a delicate approach when addressing sensitive topics with your spouse, try anyway. Practice is called practice for a reason, and you will get plenty of practice here.

Avoid Debating Their Feelings

Responses to your spouse's feelings should not be rebuttals. This is not a debate. Your response to their feelings during this entire process should be with the intent to connect, appreciate, enrich, or correct. The verbal spirit of your response will be, "I hear you," followed by repeating what you believe you heard. That's called connecting. Then you can continue in appreciation, "Thank you for seeing that in me," or growth, "I understand; how can I be better for us?" or correction, "What can we do together to make this better for us?"

Be Open to Help

There may be times when there are no answers, and sometimes the best answer to "What can we do to make this better for us?" will be "I don't know, yet." That "yet" is a word of intent. It allows you to complete this book and potentially seek counseling help when the need arises. Conflict may happen, disagreements may ensue, and fear may grip you. These are all common occurrences when the norm or the status quo is being challenged. You will want to give up on the process because it will seem too hard to face or too big to face alone. Don't give up. Get help.

Disclaimer

Physical, emotional, and verbal abuse all make a marriage unsafe and we sincerely pray that this is not the state of your marriage. If it is, we encourage you to seek immediate help. This book alone will not help in these areas. Abuse is volatile and dangerous to all involved, and it's important that you understand that it will take sincere commitment to change, intense therapy, and consistent effort from both spouses if your marriage is to be saved from this.

Note for Small Group Leaders

As small group leaders, your role is to guide and moderate. While we understand that you may have a passion and wisdom in many facets of marriage, we want you to guide rather than counsel couples in your small group setting. Through observation, we want you to monitor the couples for a sense of unresolved distress between them. When you sense this, don't jump to a conclusion; take time with them outside of the meeting to make sure your sense is correct. Whenever issues go beyond your ability to help or soothe couples in distress, consult your pastor for further guidance.

Note for Small Group Leaders

Create a Safe Environment for Everyone

When moderating the group, you're allowing couples to engage with the material. It's important that you encourage questions and interaction while maintaining a safe and positive environment for everyone. Never allow couples to use discussion opportunities to embarrass, damage, vilify or "out" their spouses in meetings. Encourage each couple to agree on what can and cannot be shared before speaking publicly about each other. If there is anything to be kept private, make sure that couples are still having the important conversations at home and reporting their results and progress to the group.

As the small group leader, your job is to keep the conversation flowing and make sure that the opportunity to share and speak is available to everyone. You're the ice-breaker and the tie-breaker. You must establish a warm atmosphere for everyone and transition conversation when it's time to move forward.

Maintain Control of The Environment

There may be couples who will try to use the small group as their personal group counseling session, and it's important to discourage couples from doing this. Perhaps they've had a big fight or a pillar has recently been broken and they need to talk through it. If this happens, deal with the couple away from everyone else. Pray with them, and then ask both couples if this is something that they want to have the group pray for. This alleviates embarrassment and facilitates trust in you as a leader. While some members of the group will want to offer their help, guidance, or support, it's important that this help is constructive. Additionally, always make sure that you can provide resources for extra help. Those resources may be a particular pastor, a counselor, books, or other materials.

Everyone Matters

We understand that there are some people who will share and others who will be a bit more reserved. Be careful not to allow one couple to usurp or hog all the time during the meetings. These situations allow for extended amounts of time for some couples while leaving others out. Moderate the time so that you can maintain a healthy tone for your small group. In that same vein, don't force anyone to share if they are not comfortable. Some will need time to open up, and that's okay.

Set Up a System of Accountability

Accountability is key in small groups, and we don't want this to be any different. Commit to coming to each meeting changed with a pillar intact. Check in on couples to be sure they are doing the work and hold them accountable to their word to cover their spouse.

With that said, let's get started.

The 4-Pillars

...Upon This Rock

Within every community or circle of friends, there will never be a shortage of relationship advice. There will be those who have read all of the best books, those who "know it all" simply because they've lived it all, and those who will always recommend the best therapists because they themselves had to go through a few to find the right one. Someone everywhere will always have you covered.

Within those same groups, however, there will also be couples who have tried everything. There will be those who have read all of the books that friends recommended, those who have attended marriage conferences and retreats with hopes of healing and change, or those who have gone to counseling that didn't seem to do anything but leave them more frustrated in the end. We know because we've been there...on both sides.

As life-long students of all things love and relationships, we too have done our fair share of research on what makes love and relationships work and what causes them to break down over time. This ranges from discovering and defining your *Love Language* (Dr. Gary Chapman) to understanding *His Needs and Her Needs* (Dr. Willard F. Harley) to giving and receiving Love and Respect (Dr. Emerson Eggerichs) all the way down to asking ourselves, "What went wrong in our own failed relationships and marriages?" We have traced and tracked the key relationship influencers that both build and break relationships, and what we have found is that nearly all of these amazing resources encompass the need for variations (in one form or another) of what we refer to as the *4-Pillars*.

We define marriage pillars as the upright, load-bearing structures that are designed to support the weight of your relationship. These pillars protect the relationship so that it is unmoved or unshaken by outside conditions. While the foundation of a relationship is built with love, friendship, admiration, and respect, it is the things that are built upon that foundation—and reinforced over time—that we refer to as the *4-Pillars of Marriage*. These *4-Pillars* stand on that foundation and support the weight of your active covering while preserving your marriage as a sanctuary for those inside. No matter what earth-shaking situation arises, the pillars hold the foundation in place and keep the covering intact. Without these pillars, the roof falls in, the foundation cracks, and the veil of your marriage is ripped from top to bottom. Your marriage is sacred. Your marriage is a sanctuary. Without the pillars in place, your marriage is left exposed and unprotected.

Love Isn't Enough

The *4-Pillars* that we will introduce in this book will not be based on concepts unheard of. All of the terms or "pillars" will be very familiar to you in theory. However, as obvious as they *should* be, we have not found any books or research that explores the need for these pillars specifically, all in one place. Much of the research alludes to these pillars in one way or another but stops short of giving them a name and significance in today's marriage landscape.

Many books and marriage resources explore love, selflessness, communication (conflict), and sex. These are the glaring and obvious needs that many seek in a marriage, and they are usually the first lines of defense when trying to repair the brokenness within it. However, couples who love each other file for divorce every day, just as there are couples who still enjoy sex but have no idea how to communicate or resolve conflicts. This is because love or sex alone does not create an environment for intimacy or a healthy relationship. Being able to solve conflict alone doesn't build or enhance intimacy and connection. So, we contend that the song was wrong when it said, "All You Need is Love." It takes more. Building the construct of a healthy relationship is an intentional study and application of key behaviors that nearly every relationship craves, four of which you will find within this book.

What This Book and the 4-Pillars Will Do for Your Marriage

This will not be a book that shows you how to "fight better." We will not be providing tips on how to reignite sex in your marriage. And while we will introduce ways to connect and communicate within the *4-Pillars*, we will not be teaching you new and improved methods to talk to one another. This book is about building or rebuilding your relationship "house," beginning with repositioning yourselves as each other's covering and reinforcing your home by adhering to these pillars.

You will learn how to become a place of refuge for your spouse in a way that allows them to explore and express who they are with you. You will learn how to protect your marriage from anything or anyone outside of your marriage that threatens the stability of your relationship. You will explore ways of recovering your marriage if any of these pillars have been breached, broken, or eroded over time. And finally, you will learn how to feel and heal each other in ways that will allow you to reopen the doors of friendship and intimacy.

This book will change your mind about much of what you thought you knew about marriage. It will dispel myths of what a happy marriage is supposed to look like, and it will establish a new paradigm for how you see each other and your own marriage moving forward. We will give practical tips and exercises for each pillar, as well as provide examples from our own lives and marriage so that you and your spouse can see living examples of what these pillars look like in action.

Our prayer is that this book enriches your friendship, tightens your partnership, and strengthens your marriage. May you see each other more clearly and cover each other more completely with each pillar.

The 4 Pillars and Your Past

As we dive into each pillar separately throughout this book, it's important for you to be gut-level honest and bring all that you are into this process of discovery. For many, these pillars will be foreign, not because you have never heard of the concept of any of the pillars before, but because some of your pasts have shaped you with distorted perceptions of what each pillar means.

From traumatic childhood experiences to toxic adult relationships, each event in your past plays an important role in who you are today, as well as who you are within your marriage. Sometimes, we are unable to provide security to our spouse because events in our lives have left us insecure in ourselves. For some, parental relationships have disrupted our ability to trust people in our own interpersonal relationships. If our personal experiences with these pillars have been built on an emotionally unhealthy foundation, then the success of our marriage depends on our ability to unlearn some of these habits and perceptions.

While we do want this book to challenge you and some of the mentalities that may be harming your marriage, we also want it to serve as a launching pad for healing as well. So if while reading this book you begin to uncover a deeper need to unlearn habits of the past that threaten the safety, security, trust, or empathy of you or your marriage, then we ask that you be open to the idea of help through a third party and trusted counselor. There is nothing wrong with you and there is no judgement in becoming the best possible person that you can be for the sake of your marriage and your family.

We Are Praying For You.
We are Rooting For You.

The Martin's

Introduction

I can remember it like it was yesterday.

On the heels of a failed marriage, and with two teenage daughters seeing first-hand what toxic love looked like, I was determined to never open myself up (or them) to the potential for hurt and heartbreak again.

Kenyon Martin was, at best, a friend. At most, he was the first person to help me understand what God's design for grace and love was...and what it was not. Minute by minute, week by week, our long-distance friendship blossomed into something different than I had ever experienced before. Without ever meeting in person, his presence was constant. His voice was sure. His countenance was protective. His being was a shelter.

And then one night, while on one of our endless conversations about God, our past, and relationships, Kenyon said to me, "You need a covering. You should let me cover you."

I said, "Okay…"

What made me say that? What made me tell her that she needed a covering? What made me believe that I was the man for the job?

The truth is that, in Taccara, I saw a wife who was never married to a real husband. She fought for her place, for her voice, and even for her life. She was a wife who was never covered, and I was simply a man falling in love with someone I was willing to fight for.

With me, she would have a voice. With me, she would have a place. With me, she would be safe to be who she was, unhindered. And, ultimately, that's what I wanted: Taccara, unhindered and unfiltered. I made a decision that, if she let me, anyone who came for her had to come through me *first*. I would cover her. And so it began the moment she said, "Okay."

Love Unfiltered

It's likely no secret that Kenyon and I come ridden with experiences of abandonment, abuse, and hurt. So when people ask how long we dated before we got married, we always make the joke that we dated for all of 37 seconds. If we're honest, we didn't date much at all. We spent the time that most people use to go on dates and wear masks actually studying each other—unfiltered.

We had already dated plenty in our pasts and had no interest in waiting for any more "shoes to drop" in relationships. We wanted the real *deal*. So we bared our ugly truths to each other, bit-by-bit, as if we were waiting for the other to give up and run the opposite direction in terror and fear.

"I can be an a****** at times," Kenyon said.
"I can be a b**** sometimes," I replied.
"I'm an introvert and I like my bubble."
"I can spend an entire day on the couch, not say a single word

to anyone, and be at total peace!"
"I need a lot of attention."

And when it seemed that he was open to receiving just about everything about me that I threw at him, I hit him with the coup de grâce when I said, "Well, I snore."
He said, "Me too..."

In those early moments of our relationship, we established the core foundation for what would eventually become our marriage pillars: *safety, security, trust,* and *empathy.* If something made us uncomfortable, we said it. If we needed something from the other, we expressed it. If we had insecurities, we shared them. If we needed to be vulnerable, we left room for it.

The key to beginning the relationship this open was not expecting each other to fix these areas of fear or discomfort. We did, however, expect the person we hold closest to us to guard those intimate places. When we guard our partners' fears, hopes, dreams, and, yes, their insecurities, we are effectively shielding them from exposure to hurt, harm, or danger. In essence, we cover them.

What is a Covering?

In the Bible, there are roughly 40 different words translated as cover or covering. This ranges from the practical use for clothing to the more circumstantial use of making something secret. Among these meanings, you'll find that the general theme is to hide, protect, and present. A covering within a marriage hides the most private and intimate parts of your spouse and relationship. As their covering, you conceal any exposed areas of your spouse and marriage while protecting them from outside elements.

God's relationship to us has demonstrated what a covering looks like. In Genesis, we find Adam and Eve dealing with a newly developed sense of insecurity and shame due to their indiscretions. We see them attempt to cover themselves through hiding. Since their efforts were inadequate, God covered them in what would be the first sacrifice. He hides them from their apparent transgression, protects them from immediate condemnation, and presents them as a part of His salvific plan. From this plan came the ultimate covering of Jesus the Christ, the Anointed One, who hides our imperfections and inadequacies and presents us as faultless to a perfect God.

Hiding
Protecting
Presenting

Covering is an aspect of duty in your marital relationship. You have sacred access to your spouse. You see each other. You see the accomplishments and successes. You see your spouse's faults and transgressions. You are a sanctified and appointed covering for your spouse. This book will demonstrate how to become this for them.

Safety

My father was a creative man. He loved the arts, loved to draw, and was an expressive writer. When I was a young man, I would have loved to know the depth of my father's creativity, but that side of my father was hidden from me. He enlisted to fight in the Vietnam War to escape the abuse in his household and the war within his family. He returned from Vietnam to a world that required him to be this strong caricature of a man despite what he had faced in his youth and abroad. His vulnerability was unwelcomed, and his creativity was misunderstood, so the only place my father felt safe was in a bottle.

It wouldn't be until after my father's passing that I found pieces of him and his honesty buried deep in my grandmother's keepsakes. I found his art, I found his words, and I found his truth. It was hard to reconcile this truth with the memories of my father because I didn't recognize the man I had found. I had never gotten the privilege of knowing that man. All my life, I had only known the man who worked hard for his family. I had only known the man who fought these invisible yet tangible wars of fear, insecurity, and irrelevance. He was the man who married a strong woman yet struggled with his own strength. He was never given room to be himself because he wasn't allowed. He was never fully embraced by the people closest to him.

Whether it was a result of his generation's culture, his child abuse, the war, or his personal insecurities, what I ultimately realized was that my father felt unsafe to be himself. He was a sensitive artist who felt his emotions deeply, yet the slightest display of vulnerability or sensitivity was instantly rejected. He walked in constant fear of being seen for all that he was because being seen like that was counter-cultural to what being a "strong man" looked like. It is this kind of fear that demonstrates a lack of safety.

We all enter into relationships with similar fears. We fear that if we are seen fully, we might be rejected. We fear that if we open our hearts and deepest selves to someone, they will not find us acceptable. We fear being exposed, unwanted, and unloved by the person closest to us. We fear invisibility, insignificance, and being unheard. This fear is a human response to our innate desire to be loved and received for who we are.

Whether you realize it or not, your spouse is subject to these same fears. Layer by layer, they have opened themselves up to you, hoping you will not cringe at the sight of them. Your actions and attitude towards them in these moments will either confirm or release them from their fears.

The Pillar of Safety - Safety is actively receiving your whole spouse. It is receiving their complexities, frailties, strengths, and idiosyncrasies without question. It gives your spouse the ability to bring to you their dreams, successes, flaws, and mistakes without fear. Safety grants your spouse the freedom to remain open to you without them feeling ashamed or rejected by you. In safety, you receive your spouse for who they are and who they are becoming.

Cultivating safety in your marriage requires you to become a living sanctuary for your spouse. You are your spouse's place of naked peace and their home base. You assure them of intimate connection with no rejection. There should never be places in your marriage where your spouse feels like they have to hide from you (proverbially or literally). Safety gives your spouse the ability to be confident in you, even when they aren't confident in themselves.

In this chapter, we are going to examine four areas of safety that threaten marriage but usually go unaddressed. We'll introduce these areas with the following questions: Are they safe to be themselves? Are they safe to make mistakes? Are they safe to have a voice? Are they safe from outside influences? We will explore what each question means and how they relate to the stability of your marriage. The ultimate goal is to become or maintain a place of safety for each other.

"The Enemy of Safety is Secrecy"

Are They Safe To Be Themselves?

One weekend, Taccara and I decided to take the family out bowling. We're not bowlers, but we wanted to do something different instead of being the introverts that we are and just sitting at home. Having insight into her past, I knew that this activity bared a few scars for her because bowling was the sport of choice for an abusive ex. So, while the outing was a good way to create memories for our new blended family, it was also an opportunity to reaffirm her comfort with me without being triggered by the past.

Everyone was having a blast. Our kids (Taccara's two girls and my two boys) were talking and having a good time singing to the music. At the same time, being the nerd that I am, I was getting a crash-course in bowling via YouTube (yes, I *nailed* it). And Taccara? She was enjoying herself, too. Energetic, excited, and loud—boy, was she LOUD!

For the sake of this story, it's important to keep in mind that I'm not a loud person. I'm a watcher. I love to relax in the quiet corners of a room because it's a great vantage point to enjoy watching people. I enjoy seeing people live, grow, and have a good time. However, because I am this way, I like very little attention drawn to me. So imagine my discomfort when I look over my shoulder and see that my beautiful wife, my other half, is getting her nitty gritty boogie on in the middle of our bowling lane (insert face-palm emoji)! Of course, this draws an uneasy amount of attention in our direction.

Taccara looked up to see me looking at her, with me wearing a bland straight face. She immediately stopped dancing. Her facial expression was apologetic as if her eyes and mouth were gesturing "sorry." She then walked over to me and asked, "Are you okay? Is that too much?"

There it was. The fear trigger. The fear of her not feeling like it was okay to be herself. The fear of personal disapproval that would lead to being intimately rejected. She had been berated for so long that she was literally nervous about being herself, which, for her, translated into being "too much" for me. She was worried about being rejected in public, being rejected with the family watching, and being rejected by me.

Knowing how she was feeling, I didn't cover up my discomfort or lie to her. I gave her a real answer. *Yes*, her energy was high for me. Yes, she was wild. Yes, I was extremely embarrassed! But despite all of those feelings, no, it wasn't too much! She wasn't too much. I *loved* seeing her enjoy herself, even if I got caught in the crossfire of her joy. I genuinely loved seeing Taccara free, at peace, and confident in herself and us as a couple.

This level of acceptance was completely new to my wife. I loved her discovering that there is nothing that she could do that would make me push her away. I loved her knowing that I enjoyed her just the way that she was, and that I didn't care who was watching. I loved her coming into the knowledge that she had a real husband who protects and honors her individuality, as well as our unity. I became her safe place.

It is extremely crucial for your spouse to be received as they are. It can't be just receiving what you like about them, but you must receive everything in them and about them. Can you accept their quirks, their flaws, the days they aren't so brilliant, or the days they aren't so handsome or beautiful? Can you accept that they may not be as popular, dynamic, busy, or showy as you'd like? Can you accept their good and their bad? As the song goes, "Sunny days, everybody loves them, but tell me, baby, *can you stand the rain*?" Pardon the *New Edition* reference, but it fits. Are they safe to be their most honest selves with you?

Without Expectation

Whenever we sit with a newly engaged couple, we have honest conversations that are designed to expose everything that each of them is bringing to the table of their relationship (their habits, ideas, traditions, and home culture). These are all things that will create their expectations in marriage. In many cases, they either have no clue or haven't thought about the expectations that they have. Everything that has contributed to who you are as a person has also contributed to the expectations you may have for your spouse. It's as if your life's experiences have created a subconscious blueprint of how you believe your life should be:

- **Your Parents** - Their disposition, behavior and mannerisms (e.g. demonstration of affection, career choices, division of house chores, household hierarchy, etc.).
- **Your Belief System** - Your personal morals, values, and ethics that you've learned and come to share in your home.
- **Your Faith** - Your religious understanding, affiliation, and participation.
- **Your Conflict Style** - How your family dealt with conflict in the home and with others (e.g. confrontation, violence, passive aggression, talked through issues healthily, sought therapy when warranted, cut people off, etc.).

- **Racial Heritage** - Values, ideas, philosophies, and ethics developed by one's experience within a particular race. That experience includes history (civil, ethnic, national), current social interactions, stated or unstated prides, aesthetics, colloquialisms, etc.

- **Role Assumptions** - How you envisioned a spouse's role, such as what they do in the home, what they do at work or for work, how you manage chores and financial responsibilities, sex and intimacy (who initiates and how), etc.

- **Your Marital "Brand"** - Your imagined perception of your spouse and how they are supposed to reflect you. How you imagined they should look or how you want them to act like for the sake of appearances. The motivations, ambitions, and drive that you want your spouse to display. The image that you imagined your spouse would or should promote on your behalf for the public, etc.

Most expectations are formed out of the collection of our own experiences. The problem with this is that we are not alone in our marriage. When we expect our spouse to replicate our experiences or be molded into our personal ideas, we make it unsafe for them to be themselves by requiring them to abandon who they are. This could be the husband who thinks his wife should stay home with the kids because his mother stayed home with him as a child, the wife who desires her husband to serve in ministry leadership because she has always wanted to be married to a minister, the husband who shuts down and gives the silent treatment in conflict, or the wife who believes in talking problems through no matter how difficult things get. Many people are holding their partners to expectations that their partners have either never heard of or never agreed to.

Whether or not it is intentional, and whether or not you have their best interest at heart, it is within these expectations that your spouse will begin to feel rejected by you. Your unmet expectations will turn into criticism, and they will begin to feel like they are not enough. They will begin to withdraw because your actions will be a statement that they are not who you want. This is not to be confused with the commitment to growth, development, and evolution of and for each other. You should expect and encourage growth in one another. But if you've entered into marriage with the idea of, "once we get married, [insert, ideas, behaviors, mannerisms you don't like] will change," the mentality is laced with rejection based on your expectations.

It's important to understand that a marriage like yours has never existed before in the history of mankind. It should not look like your parents'. It should not even look like your pastors'. And while your old ideas, habits, or norms can influence your marriage, they cannot carry it. You and your spouse ought to be a unique amalgamation of your shared differences. It should be okay for your husband or wife to be who they are. You're not there to mold them into your image. Together, you should be creating something and someone new.

As for Taccara? She still gets loud, she still dances in public, and she still enjoys herself wherever we are. She is full of quirks, features, talents, habits, and ways of thinking that are very different from mine. But I don't simply tolerate her, I celebrate her. I thank God daily that her spice brings out the depth of my flavor. Our partnership is built on receiving each other whole.

Safe to Be Themselves Exercise & Discussion Questions:

1. Describe your spouse's personality. Write down their quirks, idiosyncrasies, and habits. Write down the things that make you smile and even the things that get on your nerves. Be nice. *This is meant to be light and fun.*
2. Do you feel like your spouse is safe to be their "naked self" with you without rejection?
3. What does your spouse do to let you know it's okay to be yourself?
4. Is there anything about you that you withhold from your spouse out of fear of rejection? *I.e. dreams, goals, ailments, hobbies, etc.*
    a. If so, why?
    b. Set aside some time to discuss with them.
5. Do you ever feel like your spouse is holding you to expectations that you never agreed to? If so, write down these expectations. Then, when you and your spouse designate time to discuss this, ask them where these expectations come from.
6. Do you ever feel like you are not enough for your spouse? If so, why or how?

Are They Safe To Make Mistakes?

No one is perfect, and nothing in life can ever prepare you for the level of imperfection that you will observe in your spouse. When it comes to your spouse making mistakes, what was once cute and endearing can become aggravating and insulting, especially when those mistakes are repeated over and over again. In marriage, it's easy to translate repeated mistakes as personal offenses against you. Being safe to make mistakes involves extending your spouse the grace to be imperfect without the risk of retribution.

An environment where a spouse cannot make mistakes without being criticized or ridiculed is an unhealthy one. It creates a type of anxiety that will cause them to fear disappointing you. And because they are human, it is inevitable that they will disappoint you again. When your spouse feels like they are unable to be human around you, they will become experts at avoiding you.

Taccara can get on my very last nerve. She will go into the kitchen, make a sandwich, and walk away. She will leave every single thing out on every counter. Mayo is left out. Lettuce is out, too. Not to mention the bread, lunch meat, and knife—it's all there! I don't have to ask what kind of sandwich she made because I can just go into the kitchen, do a 360-degree turn, and put the picture together. This grates on my last nerve.

The first few times, I politely asked her to clean up after herself. After I noticed that asking nicely didn't work, I asked her—no, I *told* her a little more sternly. I got loud, my voice got deeper, and I even slammed a few cabinets in protest, hoping that would motivate some change. It did a little, but I'd be lying if I said she still doesn't leave a mess in the kitchen. Now, I don't say a word. I'll pick an item up, walk into her office, and say, "Is this you?" She'll say yes, apologize, and then smile or laugh. I'll smile back and shake my head like, "Lord, this woman you gave me here?" Her actions still frustrate me, but I don't penalize her for my frustrations.

It is extremely easy to get offended when we translate our spouse's mistakes into statements. When important things get missed or when our requests get ignored repeatedly, it's easy for us to begin to tell ourselves that their actions (or lack of action) are a personal attack against us. Trust me. I've been there. When Taccara repeatedly leaves food out on the counter, I've thought things like, "She doesn't care! She doesn't respect me! She must want to poison me because she left the mayo out!" With her mother (who lives with us) right in the next room, I'd be thinking, *"Who raised you?"* It's funny now, but I used to be offended. What helped change my disposition is my ability to rethink how I was translating her actions.

It's important to understand that we are not excusing mistakes or making them okay. We are not releasing your spouse from the accountability of growth and correction. What we are trying to do is help you see your spouse's mistakes from a lens other than offense. Before ranting or harping on the issue, consider them. Are they stressed? Are they frustrated? Are they juggling too many things at once? Are they just forgetful? Look into them and their inner world to determine if maybe something is going on with them. When you shift concerns from you to them, you make it safe for them because you are trying to "see" them despite their mistakes. After that, you can find ways to work on the situation together. This includes sharing how their mistakes make you feel, regardless of how insignificant it may seem to them.

When faced with your spouse making a mistake, here's how to handle your feelings before allowing offense to cloud your emotions:

1. **Don't Boil or "Stew"** - Sitting and marinating in your aggravation will overtake your imagination. You'll be driven to draw conclusions that aren't there. You'll feel "truths" and defend them as if they were really true. If you can't address your spouse from a healthy perspective, address the immediate corrections for the situation and wait to talk to your spouse later.

    Give yourself at least 20 minutes before you talk to them. Don't think about the issue for those 20 minutes. Instead, go redirect your frustrations elsewhere and then come back to the conversation. This time will allow you and your biology to reset so that you can speak from a respectful place.

2. **Capture Every Thought** - This takes effort because negative thoughts and assumptions about your spouse

will arise effortlessly. When it comes to your spouse, pay attention to how you think about them. You'll be surprised at how often you will hear your mind portraying them as criminals and assigning them motives that hurt you.

Capturing your negative thoughts requires you to be mindful about not just what enters your thoughts, but what you allow to stay. When negative thoughts or accusations come, you will have to mentally say to yourself, "I haven't talked to them. I don't know what they're thinking. It's unfair for me to think for them." They at least deserve the right to a fair and speedy trial! Whatever you say to yourself, make sure that it detaches you from your mental accusations of them.

Also, consider the idea that offense is the default feeling of being attacked. Offense is a response to threat and fear— fear of what they really think about you, fear of being disrespected, fear of being humiliated, etc., capturing those fearful thoughts can keep you from being unsafe for them.

3. **Choose to Think Better of Your Spouse** - Negative thoughts about your spouse's intentions expose your distrust in them. It shows that you don't believe they have your best intentions at heart. So, in the spirit of capturing your thoughts, you need to check yourself on how you think about your spouse. Then choose to think better about them. What if they didn't have a negative motivation? What's another reason they may have done what they've done? Why are they continuing to forget? Is it their health? Is it stress? Is it a habit? Is it you? This

is how you become safe for them to make mistakes.

4. **Give Them the Opportunity to Correct Their Mistakes-** While it's important to have honest conversations with yourself about your spouse's mistakes, it's equally as important to have conversations with them about how their mistakes make you feel. No matter how big or small, if it's bothering you, it should be addressed. Once you address them (honestly, not brutally), allow them the time, space, and patience to grow and improve. It's easy to see when they are missing things, but put the effort into noticing them trying to do better as well. Make sure they know that you see their efforts. A little thanks goes a long way.

5. **Appreciate Their Mistakes** - Once you've settled down, captured your thoughts, and chosen to think better about your spouse, see your husband's or wife's truth. Perhaps what causes them to make that mistake is the same reason why they are so good in a different area of life. Yes, they're forgetful, but they're also always remembering things that even you'd forget. See, understand, and appreciate who your spouse is in those mistakes, and then cover their blind spots where they may miss the mark.

Taccara moves fast. She gets things done. Her mind is always laser focused on a task. When she eats, it's because her hunger is inconvenient and gets in the way of her making things happen. Without that crazy focused energy, I wouldn't love her. It's sexy to me. We are successful because of her relentless and tireless output. That's who she is when she makes those mistakes. She's not perfect, and I'm not either. She has to have room to move and be imperfect, just like I require the same room. It is entirely unfair to demand grace and then not give grace in return. She's safe with me, and I'm safe with her too.

Mistakes vs. Transgressions

At this point, some may be thinking, "Kenyon and Taccara, I get it. But what about the big mistakes that are disrespectful, neglectful, abusive, or damaging to our marriage? How do we receive our spouse after mistakes like these?"

These are not just mistakes; these are transgressions. The word transgression in the Bible means to break or violate trust. Transgressions break covenants, break hearts, and break the 4-Pillars of covering. Receiving someone after a cataclysmic transgression like adultery, abuse, addictions, or other destructive deeds will take more than the safety to make mistakes. There must be steps towards healing, repair, and change for both parties. We will address how to begin this process later in the book.

Safe to Make Mistakes Exercise & Discussion Questions:

1. Think about a common or consistent mistake that your spouse makes that drives you crazy. Write it down.
2. Why does this mistake bother you so much? How does it make you feel? Do you take it personally?
3. How do you react when your spouse makes this mistake?
4. But, did you die? Asking for a friend (your spouse). *Sorry. We're joking (sort of, answer anyway.)*
5. Have you ever spoken to them about how it makes you feel when they do this?
    a. If yes, have you noticed them trying to do better in this area? And if so, did you acknowledge them trying?
6. When your spouse makes these mistakes, is it possible that they have other things going on that may be causing them to miss things?
    a. If you're not sure, talk about it. There may be a situation that warrants a little more grace in an area.
7. Are there any mistakes that you consistently make that your spouse extends you grace and understanding for? *Be honest. Write it down.*

Are They Safe To Have a Voice?

Unless your marriage was arranged, it's safe to assume that both of you are in this marriage because you chose to be here, and every day, you choose your husband or wife all over again. There should be no greater honor in marriage than the honor of knowing that, out of all the people in the world, your spouse chose and continues to choose you. Nothing disenfranchises that choice quite like your spouse feeling as if they do not have a voice in your marriage and life together.

Being safe to have a voice means giving your husband or wife the right of consideration or influence when it comes to all matters in your lives. This means you value each other's needs, insights, and opinions regarding any and all circumstances. It doesn't mean that you will always agree, nor should this invalidate your point of view. What we are saying is that there should never be a place in your marriage where your spouse is made to feel like their voice is not considered or valued.

Friends of ours, Jacob and Mari, had been married for five years when one day Jacob came home and said, "My brother is going to stay with us for a while. He's moving to the city, and I promised I would help him out. I figure I'll just fix up the garage so he can have his own space and be out of your way." Mari just stood there blinking erratically, straight-faced and stunned. Jacob had made decisions like this in the past, but so far, the biggest "surprise" he had brought home was a car. This was definitely bigger.

Mari was furious. She immediately began to get flooded with emotions. Her feelings swung from the anxiety and stress of having to "make room" for another adult in their small house to feelings of hurt and being disrespected by her husband for not taking her feelings or thoughts into consideration. He had an entire conversation about moving someone into their home and where they would sleep without ever asking her how she felt. When she tried to express her discomfort with the situation, Jacob ignored her. When she attempted to at least lay down some ground rules in terms of his brother's contribution to the house and how long she felt it appropriate to let him stay, Jacob made her feel like she was being cold and heartless. Here she was preparing to have her family's life flipped upside down, and she had no say in the matter. Her voice was effectively disregarded by her husband.

It's humiliating for someone to feel like their voice is disregarded in their marriage. They feel insignificant when decisions are made without them, when they are never consulted, and when their opinions and needs are overlooked. Remember, your spouse chooses you every day. By not honoring their choice and removing their significance, you are devaluing their voice.

Husbands

Marriage is harder than ever for men to adjust to. We grew up with the idea that men are in charge. We are supposed to go to work, pay bills, and then come home to a clean house and a home-cooked meal. We saw our fathers and grandfathers do it. Depending on the age, it was on TV, too. Men ran the house, men had the last say, and women dealt with it. What makes marriage harder for men to adjust to today is that we are literally having to retrain our brains to see not just marriage differently, but our place and our voice in marriage differently. More than ever, men are having to learn that marriage is more about partnership and consideration than it is about a domestic dictatorship. This level of partnership is not something that many men have experienced or been taught before.

Taccara and I are traditional in that we believe in "roles" and we subscribe to the idea of submission within our marriage. However, we don't believe our roles were designed to demean or subjugate one over the other. We submit to one another. When I consider my wife's point of view, insight, and opinions as a partner, it is a natural response for her to not just submit to my voice but to actually desire it. My wife submits out of a personal confidence in my leadership and submission to God. Her submission does not disenfranchise her right in our relationship; instead, it simply establishes order for the relationship. She trusts me to lead, and sometimes that leadership means hearing and submitting to her voice.

When I was in the military, one of the first things we learned was rank and chain of command. In the command structure, officers (i.e. lieutenants, captains, colonels, etc.) ranked above the non-commissioned officers (NCO). According to this ranking system, the lowest ranking officer had power and leadership over the highest ranking non-commissioned officer. What this means is that there would be times where you could see a young officer, fresh and wet behind the ears, have a ranking assignment over an older, tenured, and more experienced NCO. This can sometimes create a toxic power struggle. What usually ends up happening is that the younger officers value the wisdom, influence, and experience of the ranking NCOs. Instead of disenfranchising their voice, they will go to the NCO for guidance on major decisions.

Ranking structures work when leadership is not threatened by those who know more than they do. Leadership is not intimidated by those who can do things better than they can. Leadership is accountability, not superiority. As a husband, you are a leader. You are accountable to two parties: Christ and your wife. You are accountable to Christ to be steward, caretaker, protector, lover, and priest of your wife. You are also accountable to your wife because she chose to give herself to you.

You and your wife will be on a life-long mission towards oneness. Part of keeping your wife safe is acknowledging, employing, and preserving her significance in your mission. Your wife is mission critical.

Wives

Before Kenyon and I were married, there was a lot I had to do on my own. I was raising my daughters, taking care of my mother, and working several jobs to make sure we all never went without. As an "independent woman" who never wanted to be put in a position to need a man, one of the hardest things I had to do was learn to step aside and allow my husband to be what I asked God for: my help. As a man, he has been designed to fix and to be functional for me. My need to control everything around me made him dysfunctional in my life.

If you've had to rely on yourself for any length of time, it will seem unnatural to relinquish control to your husband in some areas (also known as accepting help). Allowing your husband to be there for you, support you, and even take over some responsibilities for you is not saying that you can't do it. It's saying that you trust him to do it. When you do not allow your husband to be the help that you desire and deserve, you run the risk of muting your husband's voice and making a statement that you don't trust him to carry you. You are telling him that he's not husband enough for you, or not as good of a husband as you.

Your husband must be safe to be his own man. He will never be like your pastor, he doesn't have to do things like your father, and he should never have to "behave" as if he is your son. Allowing him to be safe to have a voice means giving him the opportunity to lead and grow at the same time. It's giving him the space to be a guiding voice in decisions and being able to be open to you when he doesn't have all the answers. It's using your voice to uplift him, even when he's made a mistake. It's allowing him to vent his frustrations and fears without the fear of appearing weak to you. You hold his heart. You carry his secrets. You are his safe place.

Voicing Your Needs

Both you and your spouse have needs that only a husband or wife can fulfill. Providing a safe place where your spouse can expose their needs to you is one of the most intimate acts you can perform for each other. The ability to open your heart to their needs, their desires, and their passions to you, while you respond to them with a willingness to fulfill those needs, has the ability to transform your love like never before. This will take practice.

Couples become the most selfish about having their own needs and desires met when they believe they can no longer trust their spouse to meet their needs. This happens over time, and it's likely not intentional, but the power struggle of "you vs. me" begins right there. From forgetting simple things to neglecting their basic need for touch, your spouse will learn to become independent of you if you have gone deaf to their needs.

Practice becoming a safe place for them to voice their needs; then practice meeting them.

Safe to Have a Voice Exercise & Discussion Questions:

1. Consider Jacob and Mari's situation. What do you think was the biggest issue with how the situation with Jacob's brother was handled? *Discuss your thoughts among yourselves.*
    a. Jacob didn't ask Mari for permission before inviting his brother to stay.
    b. Jacob didn't talk to Mari to see how she felt about a house guest.
    c. Mari wasn't understanding enough to Jacob's brother's situation.
    d. There was nothing wrong with the situation at all.
2. At what point should Jacob have discussed his brother's situation with Mari?
    a. As soon as the idea came up with his brother.
    b. Once he decided where his brother was going to sleep.
    c. He brought it up at the right time
3. Do you and your spouse discuss major and minor decisions before "pulling the trigger" on them? *Why or why not?*
4. Where has your spouse's voice been the most valuable to you?
5. Are there any areas where you feel like your consideration, insight, involvement, or opinion aren't welcomed?
    a. Why do you feel that way?
    b. What did they do to make you feel that way?
    c. Ask your spouse if how you feel is the truth. (That should have a yes or no answer.)

Safe to Have a Voice Exercise & Discussion Questions Continued:

6. Are there any areas where you feel like you and your spouse could do better at considering each other's voices?
7. Do you feel safe in voicing your needs to your spouse? *Why or why not? (e.g. Have they shut your needs down in the past? Has it been a long time since they've had a desire to meet your needs? Talk about this together.)*
8. Do you feel as if your spouse hears and responds to your needs?

Are They Safe From Outside or Competing Influences?

This is the last focal point of the pillar of safety: safe from outside influences. This tends to be a sensitive subject because it requires letting go. You must let go of assumed loyalties and allegiances as well as relationships that do not honor the sacred position of your husband or wife. This challenges husbands and wives to actually leave and cleave. We're not only speaking about parents, but we're referring to anyone outside of the husband-and-wife relationship. Your spouse must know that you will protect them from all enemies, both foreign and domestic. Anyone who challenges the authority, relevance, and priority of your spouse becomes an enemy to your relationship.

You both are the nucleus to a new, living organism called your marriage. As the nucleus, you are responsible for regulating your environment and ensuring that it stays healthy and safe. Every life-giving and life-preserving element of your relationship begins and ends with you. Even though you have both been part of pre-existing "organisms" or relationships already, it can be difficult to "forsake all others" without feeling like you're being disrespectful or disloyal to those who love you. From parents and pastors to childhood friends and your children, all of these relationships matter. However, once you're married, they are no longer the priority.

When we look into the Scriptures, we see the directive given to the husband to leave his father and mother and cleave, cling to, or be united with his wife (Gen 2:24; Matt 19:5; Mk 10:7; Eph 5:31). The reason why the directive appeared one-sided is because the tradition already implied that the bride-to-be would be leaving the home of her father and mother. In that culture, the bride's father was her protector and keeper. When he gave his daughter's hand in marriage, his responsibilities over his daughter were transferred to her husband. The husband took the father's place in the sense that he was now her protector and provider. Both the husband and wife became one, alone.

While the wedding day may have included both families and all of their friends, when it came time for the consummation of that marriage, everyone was outside the door of that room. That's marriage! A locked room where you are naked, exposed, and intimate, and everyone else is outside of that room. No one should be able to infiltrate this bond, disrespect your spouse, or establish a place of priority over them.

When it comes to parents, you love them, you honor them, and you have the utmost respect for them. However, the moment you said, "I do," you effectively repositioned them. They will always be parents in title, but their function cannot be one of control or authority concerning your life. They will have their own ideas, traditions, and expectations of you and your spouse, but that is none of your business. Your business is what you are establishing in your marriage.

Safety: Are They Safe Outside or Competing Influences?

Repeat after us:

> *I do not go to bed with my parents. I am not building a life with my parents. So my parents have no say in my marriage.*

When it comes to children, this may be difficult to digest, especially in matters of blended families. Your husband or wife is still the priority. We are not saying your children should be ignored, mistreated, neglected, or abandoned. What we are saying is that your children should not be competing with your spouse. Children may take a greater time commitment and may require a different type of attention. However, it's important to make sure that your spouse never feels like they are the dog getting the children's "leftovers" or crumbs from you. You show up for PTA. You show up for softball practices. You show up for bathtime. You show up for bedtime. You must also make time and an effort to show up for each other.

In blended families with children, it's important to remember that your children are your responsibility, but you are not theirs. Be sure to provide your children with the safety to express discomfort with any situation, but create the appropriate boundaries so they don't feel like they have authority over your situation. You and your spouse must establish a game plan that addresses how you will manage the blending process while keeping your relationship as a priority. For this, we recommend premarital (or post-marital) counseling with a professional that specializes in blended families.

How do we prioritize our spouse over outside influences?

1. **Consider them in your connections:** Are you connected to people who disrespect your spouse or your marriage? Do you have "friends" who disregard your spouse in their conversations with you?

2. **Consider them in your conversations:** Consider your spouse before letting anyone into your home. "Letting someone in" is both figurative and literal. Conversations or flirtations with people that would hurt your spouse or make them uncomfortable, airing the dirty laundry of your marriage, sharing intimate details of your marriage without your spouse's permission, or allowing someone to disrespect your spouse without standing up for them are all ways in which you should consider them in your conversations.

3. **Consider them in your counsel:** There may come a point in your marriage where you are in need of help. You may have friends that you like to vent to. This is normal! Considering your spouse in these instances means understanding their comfort level with who you talk to and what about. Agree on the wise counsel or mentorship for your marriage. Agree on what's okay to air without demonizing each other. Ultimately, you know when what you are saying will offend your spouse. This idea isn't as much about getting permission as it is about demonstrating consideration.

In order for your marriage to survive and thrive, you must treat it as the priority. When we allow anyone to alter our priority, then they have the ability to alter us and influence us.

Safe from Outside Influences Exercise & Discussion Questions:

1. Are there any competing influences in your marriage that could be seen as a priority over your spouse?
2. Has your spouse expressed any discomfort with anyone in your life that could be seen as an outside or competing influence? *If yes, have you had a hard time repositioning that person in your life? Why?*
3. Is there anyone you feel that your spouse prioritizes over you? *If yes, who is it? Have you expressed your discomfort with this person to your spouse? How did they respond?*
4. Do you have wise counsel or other marriage coaches that you have both agreed were safe for your marriage? *Talk about this together and discuss what you're comfortable with your spouse sharing. The goal is to find people that you don't have to censor yourself with while also maintaining respect for your spouse.*
5. Have you and your spouse agreed upon family or friends that both of you can trust to vent to? *If yes, write who.*
6. In what three ways can you start prioritizing your spouse above all others?

Establishing the Pillar of Safety

Here are four rules to live by when establishing the pillar of safety in your marriage:

1. *Shed your expectations* — Avoid allowing your expectations to alienate your spouse. Practice receiving your spouse as an individual and appreciate their differences just as much as you appreciate their similarities. You both are different, and that's okay.

2. *Live in abundant grace* — Receive your spouse in their mistakes. Love them in their effort to improve. Accept that they may disappoint you again.

3. *Relearn their voice* — Don't become so familiar with your spouse's voice that you become deaf to their needs, desires, or opinions.

4. *Establish them as a priority* — Their safety with you relies on the assurance that they are first before anyone outside of you two.

Security

It was 2am on a Sunday morning when I was suddenly awakened out of my sleep with debilitating anxiety. We had just had one of our first big fights where we had said big cuss words to each other. I was certain that what we were fighting over, and what had been said, was enough to make him rethink his decision to love me.

It was strangely quiet in the room, and I didn't hear Kenyon breathing, so I started gently feeling around his side of the bed. If he was still there, I didn't want to wake him. But I was also still mad, so I didn't want it to seem like I was checking for him, either.

As I tapped gently, closer to his side, I inadvertently touched his arm, and his still voice said, "I'm still here." In that moment, I knew that everything would be okay.

Not everyone comes from a battered or broken past, but *most* of us have had relationships that have fallen apart in those big, defining moments. The fights, unfaithfulness, or even the mismanagement of emotional or financial currency have all been known to topple many a relationship. Because I was no stranger to any of those types of occurrences in my past, I had been conditioned to believe that relationships were only built on the "loving" moments, while the big (sometimes hurtful) moments were where relationships were broken.

The truth is, these big, defining moments can either build your marriage or break it...but you do have a choice.

Kenyon never threatened to leave or displayed behavior that

threatened our marriage. Even though we had made the "I ain't goin' nowhere" promises to one another, that big fight was terrifying because the stability of those promises had never truly been tested. His position of stability in that moment was pivotal for me because it helped build my confidence in his position in our marriage. What preserved my confidence in his position was his consistency in all areas that continued to show me who he was. It was a level of security that didn't prevent us from having the big fights or conflict; it just made us less afraid of the conflict.

The Pillar of Security - Security is the atmosphere of dependability, consistency, and predictability that you create with your spouse. It gives your spouse the audacity to believe in you as you establish the emotional, physical, and financial assurances within your relationship. While the pillar of safety locks the door, security is your spouse being able to rest because they can see and experience the constant act of the door being locked by you.

There are three areas of security that we believe are pivotal to your marriage success: emotional security, physical security, and financial security. The pillar of security is a structure all on its own, but emotional, physical, and financial security are what we consider composites that add strength to the pillar and reinforces its stability. In this chapter, we will take a deeper look at these three areas of security and demonstrate how this pillar should work in your marriage.

Emotional Security

Emotional security is giving your spouse the confidence in knowing that you will be a dependable and steadfast presence in your marriage, even in their absence. It relies on your character to be who you promised them that you would be. Emotional security covers your spouse's vulnerabilities and shields their heart from hurt or danger. Emotional security may look different or have different requirements for you and your spouse, so it's important to intimately understand what your spouse will need in order to feel emotionally secured by you.

As a young girl, I was rejected by my biological father and later disowned by him. As a result, it's only natural that a large part of my sense of emotional security within my marriage is heavily rooted in the idea of knowing that my husband will not leave me when things get hard. For Kenyon, he's experienced infidelity in his past, so it is important for him to know that our relationship is secured from the danger of outside relationships. While neither of us is responsible for healing our spouse's insecurity, there is an expectation that, by disclosing our propensity for insecurity in these areas, our spouse will guard or cover our insecurities through their actions and behavior.

Since my husband has dealt with infidelity in his past, I am intentional about ensuring that he is never left unsecured when it comes to my male friendships. This means making sure he feels safe about every male friendship that I have. I make sure that he knows who they are, while also ensuring that they are respectful towards my husband. When someone calls, I give him the courtesy of letting him know who it is. When I have conversations with one of my male friends, I let him know so it's not a surprise later. We don't hide things from each other, and even though I know he won't go through my phone or my computers, he has the passwords to them all. If I allow my husband's insecurities to remain exposed, with no effort of providing safety, security, or dependability for him, then I am leaving him unsecured.

When Taccara and I first met, she let it be known that her experience with abuse and abandonment had shaped her in more ways than one. She has fears of not being received. She has fears of not being enough. And she is terrified that one day, I will wake up and see in her what everyone else did that caused them to leave her, just like her father. It's important that I provide consistent emotional security for her, *especially* during the difficult times in our marriage. I can be as mad as a box of frogs, but I won't even let an argument ensue without her knowing that I still love her and that this is nothing that we can't overcome.

When I tell her that I love her and that I'm just as committed to her when I'm mad, it demonstrates that she can rest with me without concern. This is a consistent practice that I uphold, even when I don't feel like it, because it is important for me to create an atmosphere where she is not anxious about what will happen next. I am consistent, I am dependable, and I am predictable for her, just as she is for me.

It could be that your spouse has experienced something in their past that has caused them to become insecure, and while it may not be your fault, this is a part of who they are. As their spouse, you are responsible for creating an atmosphere so that they can be secure in the fact that you will never make them repeat what has hurt them in their past. You can secure your spouse, even in their insecurity.

Being Insecure vs. Unsecured

Before we go any further, it's important to distinguish the difference between being insecure and being unsecured. Being insecure is based on your internal fears and beliefs about you, likely resulting from your past experiences. Being unsecured is being left uncovered, unprotected, or unguarded, by those closest to you.

In marriage, being unsecured happens by you exhibiting behavior that removes safety and unlocks the door to external influences in your relationship. It's allowing your spouse to live in fear of what may come next or what you will do next that will harm them in the relationship. Leaving your spouse unsecured creates a level of insecurity within them where you must establish an environment for repair. We'll address how to recover from this in the final chapter.

If you find that past insecurities are affecting your present marriage, first you must acknowledge and address your insecurities. Insecurity left unchecked can destroy your marriage because it creates a negative (and often destructive) "rewards cycle" in your relationship. For example, let's say you begin to experience insecurity about your attractiveness because you were teased as a child. Now that you are married, you worry that your spouse will one day not find you attractive anymore. One day, you get up the courage to tell them that you don't feel attractive, and, like any good spouse, they respond with how amazing you are and that you are the sexiest person in the world to them! That's the reward.

For a moment, that reward works, and you can breathe again, but later it begins to nag you some more because they *have* to say that you are sexy, right? They're married to you! So the cycle begins. Now you begin to doubt their feelings of attractiveness towards you even more, and even though they continue to be complimentary and try to make you feel good about yourself, it doesn't quite feel genuine or truthful and the compliments now only make you feel worse. But if they stop complimenting you, you begin to accuse them of not being truthful as well. This cycle will erode your marriage and cause your spouse to feel like they can do *nothing* right to love you—and they'd be right. It could also cause you to seek fulfillment outside of your marriage because you need to feel that someone who has no obligation to you finds you attractive. This is where that dangerous rewards cycle will begin again, and it will now incorporate other people. The element of insecurity can rip through your marriage like a cyclone, and it is your responsibility to find ways to silence the storm within you.

Since insecurity is internal, addressing it may involve counseling to help you uncover the root of it and then help you find healthy ways to respond to it. After you acknowledge your places of insecurity, ask your spouse to help you by creating an environment where you will feel safe. It's important that you are able to share your insecurities with them without fear or shame. This type of environment will enable you to help them understand what behaviors could cause you to feel unsecured by them.

If insecurity has been caused by your spouse's recent behavior (infidelity, mismanagement of money, abuse, etc.), then they will need to take consistent steps towards resecuring you before your insecurity dissipates, and this will take time. You will learn more about this in the final chapter, Repairing Broken Pillars.

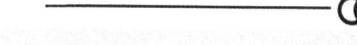

Emotional Security Exercise & Discussion Questions:

With each question, take time to flesh out and write your answers. Once you've written out each answer, set aside time to discuss each one with your spouse, not necessarily all at once. The goal of these will be to reflect on areas to work on within yourself, as well as for your spouse.

1. Has anything happened in your past (abandonment, neglect, abuse, infidelity, etc.) that has created areas of insecurity within you? If yes, write them down.

Emotional Security Exercise & Discussion Questions Continued:

2. Have you and your spouse shared the events from your past that may have created areas of insecurity within each of you? *If not, set aside some alone time to share what you wrote in question one.*

3. Are there areas where your spouse has left you unsecured in your marriage, even if it was unintentional? If yes, write them down.

4. Finish this statement: "I feel the most emotionally secure in my marriage when _____."

5. What are some ways that you can secure your spouse in your marriage? *Set aside some time to discuss what each of you wrote for question three so that you can better answer this.* **This must be a safe space for you both to speak.**

Physical Security

Physical security is the mental and emotional disposition of being physically cherished. It encompasses physical affection, physiological adaptation, and the obvious aspects of physical protection. However, physical security in marriage goes far beyond being protected from criminals and thieves. It establishes an environment that allows your spouse to be comfortable and at peace with you. One thing is for certain, physically securing your spouse includes a simple yet highly overlooked activity that many miss every day: getting physical.

Security and Physical Affection

This aspect of physical security is all about ensuring your spouse feels desired and wanted. They should never leave "hungry" for what they physically crave from you. Catering to your spouse's need for physical affection (in the way that they desire it) releases "feel-good" hormones that reduce pain and stress and stimulates a calming sensation within them. This is what security feels like. Conversely, the lack of physical affection is interpreted as rejection, and their brain is wired to respond to that rejection the same way it responds to physical pain. With each day, they experience an increased level of stress and anxiety, and their heart physically begins to hurt. They become unsecured. Even if it's unintentional, they will eventually shut down from you, just to avoid being rejected by you.

My wife's love language is physical touch. Long before she ever wanted to know if I could protect her from "bad guys," she needed to know that I could protect her heart from feeling rejected. Taccara had previously been in relationships that made her need for physical touch feel frivolous and unimportant. As a pillar of security for her, it was crucial that we cultivated places of physical security in our relationship so that we could always stay in-tune with one another. We became friends and we grew to understand what we each needed from the other when it came to physical affection. She needed my touch. I needed her kisses.

When we first met in person, I kissed her immediately. When she needed to rest, she fell asleep on my chest. After we were married, she refused to fall asleep without some piece of her body touching mine. When she feels "distant" from me, she randomly comes to me, just to give me a kiss. And whenever I notice that we are beginning to "miss" each other physically (intimately), I will let her know in no uncertain terms that I still crave her, and I want her…NOW.

Physical affection is the most sacred way that you can secure your spouse. It invites them into a place in you that no one else has access, and it perpetually reaffirms your connection to them. Even if it's not something that you are used to, even if your spouse has seemed to not need it in the past, we challenge you to practice the art of loving your spouse the way they need to be loved. It could change the entire trajectory of your marriage.

Security and Physiological Adaptation

Physiological adaptation is how the internal functions of our body respond to external stimulation like music or touch or even violence. Whether it is from the present or the past, your spouse has adapted to the environments that have shaped them. Cultivating an atmosphere of physical security in your marriage includes removing negative elements that could cause stress, anxiety, or fear in your spouse. If you both establish an environment of love, patience, kindness, understanding, and grace, that is what you both will adapt to. Your home will be a place that you are both eager to enjoy because your body responds positively by just being there. However, things like fear, aggression, passive aggression, emotional outbursts, emotional withdrawal, or even physical abuse will cause negative, physiological effects, and you will both begin to adapt to the toxicity. This environment is, at best, toxic and, at worst, abusive.

Your spouse should never be afraid of what they will encounter with you from one moment to the next. Anxiety, chronic stress, hypertension, and ulcers (to name a few) can all be byproducts of a toxic home environment that rips away its physical security. This is not to say that you won't ever get angry, that you don't have the right to be upset in your home, or that you won't ever have bad days. It's just important to recognize that you can be frustrated without belittling your spouse. You can be angry without terrorizing the home. You can have a bad day while still allowing your home environment to be fueled by love and not fear. Whatever the environment you cultivate in your home, just know that it will physiologically live with your spouse, and your children, for the rest of their lives.

If your home currently exists in a persistent toxic state, and it does not feel safe, you are encouraged to visit www.TheHotline.org. It's a safe place where you can anonymously speak to someone about your situation and learn how to move forward from here.

Physical Security Exercise & Discussion Questions:

1. What type of physical affection do you prefer most?
2. What type of physical affection does your spouse prefer most? *Hint: If you don't know, ask them. Then practice with them.*
3. How do you normally handle stressful situations in the home?
    a. Walk away and do something to regroup and collect my thoughts.
    b. Take it out on everyone around me.
    c. Self-medicate (overeating, drinking, drugs, etc.).
    d. Hold it in.
4. How do you treat your spouse when you are angry, frustrated, or irritated?
    a. Give them the silent treatment.
    b. Become silent and passive aggressive (e.g. being upset but avoiding direct communication and maintaining a disruptive silence through pouting, crass remarks or mean comments, or slamming things in frustration while maintaining "nothing" is wrong).
    c. Speak to them in a harsh tone (in words or voice).
    d. Become physically violent.
5. Have this conversation with your spouse: "Do I ever exhibit any behavior that makes you nervous or anxious?" *They must be safe to express this without any judgement, argument, or rebuttal. If the answer is yes, you both should share ways that would make the environment safer.*

Financial Security

Everyone has a different definition or concept of financial security; that's why it is so important to discuss here. This won't be a segment where we are going to teach you how to master your money habits to get rich. Instead, we want to talk about how you address money.

What we have found is that couples either do great at talking about money, don't talk about money at all, or they only discuss money when there's a big emergency and something is about to get cut off or taken away. If you're not careful, the inability to create financial security in your marriage can quickly break down every other pillar in it.

Financial security is not about Dad working until he retires and collecting a check or Mom hiding a "stash" of cash under the mattress for a rainy day. Financial security is all about protecting your home from dangers seen, unseen, and unforeseen. Dave Ramsey defines financial security as "having the money to achieve a desired standard of living now while still being able to cover emergencies and future financial goals." It doesn't matter who controls the money or who is "better" at managing it. This definition implies that couples make financial plans and contingencies together.

One of the scariest things for a couple to face is the threat of losing a home, transportation, or even electricity because of the lack of money, especially when they have a family. Creating a plan for financial security gives your spouse a peace of mind and pride in you because you both have created a plan to steward the flow of resources in the home. And you've done this as a team.

Here Are Five Key Reasons Many Couples Struggle with Finances in Their Marriage:

1. They didn't take an in-depth look at their income, debt, spending habits, and money goals before they got married.
2. They "joined together" in marriage, but not in money.
3. They have completely different approaches to money.
4. One spouse controls the money and spending while the other spouse is left in the dark.
5. One or both spouses are ashamed of their income, spending, or debt so they hide their financial situations from each other.

The greatest commonality in this list is the lack of communication. They either don't talk about money at all or they hide their money situation from their spouse altogether. Money, and how it is handled by you, is one of the most destructive secrets you can have because it leaves your spouse completely in the dark and completely unsecured. Your spouse should never have to worry or wonder if there is a catastrophe waiting for them that could pull their foundation from under them. They should never have to wonder if you will be able to take care of "your part" of the bills each month. They should never have to be afraid of what your debt has coming for them when they least expect it. And they most certainly shouldn't worry about whether or not you are hiding money or assets from them. As a safe and secured unit, you should create budgets, plans, and living wills to make sure your lives are secured with one another.

Dr. Alexandra Solomon once wrote, "When you unwrap the topic of money, you find it contains entire worlds of hidden meaning. Money and power. Money and control. Money and worthiness. Money and self-esteem. Money and love." Once you understand what money means to you, how you came to feel this way about money, and whether or not it positively or negatively impacts your money habits in your marriage, you can ensure that you are properly working to build layers of financial security in your home.

If money is a sensitive topic in your home, the financial security exercise will challenge you both because we are going to ask you to do things that make you uncomfortable. However, consider this: Your spouse washes your dirty underwear and has likely seen the worst of you, yet they still love you enough to do whatever it takes to build a life of healthy love with you— even walk through this book with you. This is your partner!

Before you begin the exercise, try to make sure your environment is safe, free from judgement, and as free of tension as possible. Let love, patience, and grace abound here.

Financial Security Exercise & Discussion Questions:

1. How does money make you feel about you? Why? What contributed to these feelings?
2. Have you and your spouse joined bank accounts? If not, why not?
3. Have you and your spouse taken an in-depth look at your income, debt, and spending habits? If not, make time to do this. If you believe it will be challenging, do it with a counselor that specializes in helping couples conquer tough conversations. A good start is to find a counselor that specializes in EFT (Emotionally Focused) Marriage Therapy.
4. Do you and your spouse have money goals for your marriage with a plan to work towards them? If not, set aside some time to discuss your money goals (e.g. how much you want to save for your kids' college, when you want to buy or pay off a home, when you want to retire, how much money you want to have at retirement, etc.).
5. Is there anything about your personal finances that you've been keeping from your spouse and that you believe will hurt them or scare them if you shared it with them? If yes, write it down.

Financial Management Resources

A. *Total Money Makeover Book by Dave Ramsey*
B. Financial Peace University, Dave Ramsey (comes with a deeper level of accountability if done through your church)
C. Every Dollar budgeting App

Establishing the Pillar of Security

Now that we've broken down the areas of security and helped demonstrate how each area should look, here are four key rules to live by when establishing the pillar of security in your marriage:

1. ***Be dependable***—in word and in deed. Be who you promised them that you'd be.
2. ***Be predictable***—Never allow your spouse to have to wonder:
   - Where you are (emotionally or physically)
   - Who they are to you
   - What they can always expect from you
3. ***Be aggressively affectionate*** every chance you get.
4. ***Approach every decision in life from the perspective of we, not me.*** Be intentional about considering them and their feelings in every decision that you make:
   - Does this decision align with our vows and our direction as a couple?
   - Will this decision hurt them?
   - Will I have to hide this decision from them?
   - Will this violate my commitment that I made to them?

Trust

As a man, it's hard to admit that, before Taccara, I had been hurt and disappointed by almost every woman I'd ever valued in my life. It was the kind of betrayal that no one should ever have to go through. When men endure something like this, it's natural for us to put up an emotional wall and believe that we will never be able to put our full faith and confidence in another woman again. And so, from then on, I had decided that I would have to protect myself and my heart from everyone, always being on guard and always obsessing about my surroundings.

As long as I was alone and not allowing anyone into my space, it was easy for me to keep my guard up and keep hurt at bay. However, humans are designed for intimate connections, and the ability to live without that intimate connection is either a gift from God, a numbing mercy, or a special kind of pain. As natural as it was for me to retreat into a place of self-preservation after hurt, the desire to give and receive love was just as natural. I still desired that human connection. I desired a confidant. I still wanted a safe place to bring down my guard and remove my emotional "armor." When I began to get serious about Taccara and allow her into my life, there was an emotional tug-of-war inside me. I wanted to trust her, but I also was afraid of allowing her to get too close where I would be exposed to potential hurt. The only way to counterbalance the fear I had was with truth.

Honesty and truth set the standard and tone for how we loved, how we worked together, and even how we prayed. Yes, even in prayer we needed to be honest. It was important that we spoke to God from a place of honesty, without our masks. As we made room for each other, we left no room for false appearances or pretenses. We actively pursued truth, because when we did, we found trust, and that trust allowed us to be safe with each other. But it wasn't enough just to feel like we could trust each other. We needed to authentically experience it in action. You'll never know the true strength of something until the capacity of its limits are tested. Then, we got married.

Have you ever walked into a crowded room and felt like all conversations stopped and everyone's eyes were suddenly on you? That's how it felt walking into a blended family with Taccara, her two teenage daughters, and her mother—all *women*. I loved Taccara, and I loved her family, but I didn't *know* them. I wasn't exactly sure of my role with them. I didn't know how to "blend in" or how to engage with them. And while I am certain that they all likely felt the same way about me, they had each other. I felt like I only had me. I stayed on guard at all times because I was quite literally a stranger in an environment that felt very familiar to what had hurt me in my past.

I watched everything—everyone's movements, actions, behaviors, and words—and since I didn't know what to expect, or whom to expect it from, all of my personal fears of betrayal caused me to react to everything around me out of that insidious distrust. Betrayal, no matter when it's experienced, comes with a certain level of PTSD that causes an extreme level of anxiety and panic in even the most emotionally solid people. As a counselor, and a man who had been educated in everything I was experiencing, it was still hard for me to see everyone around me as anything but a potential threat.

Hidden and unknown distrust in your marriage will have you walking through a minefield. When distrust is apparent, at least you know what you are dealing with and can somewhat understand how to ease it. When it's hidden or unknown, it has the potential to trigger all sorts of emotions between you both. While Taccara and I knew that our honesty early on had set the stage for an awesome marriage, we didn't prepare the same stage for our blended family. So, when we combined my latent PTSD from betrayal and Taccara's PTSD from abuse, with an environment of children and a mother that I didn't spend the same amount of time falling in love with, we had no clue that we were existing in a place where we still distrusted each other. I distrusted the idea that I could fully trust my surroundings. Taccara distrusted my reaction to my surroundings as if I was going to become like the abusers of her past. We were both on high alert. We didn't argue a lot, but whenever we did, it was against our own imaginations of each other. What helped us overcome this place of distrust was the same honesty that we started out with.

One day, I was having a phone conversation with a family member whom I was noticeably irritated with. Upon hearing the agitation in my voice, Taccara asked what were they saying that was making me so upset. "You don't get it," I said. "They're constantly calling me and pretending like they've never betrayed me yet expecting me to smile and laugh as if they don't owe me an apology!"

"Well, have you addressed it with them?" Taccara asked.
"No. There's no point. I've just resolved to get over it," I said.

"But you're obviously not over it," Taccara replied. "And if you're not going to have an honest conversation with them about it, then it's unfair of you to continue to punish them for something that you refuse to address."

OUCH!

Those words pierced me in more ways than one. Not only was I punishing this family member for something I refused to address with them, I was punishing my wife and my new family for something I was refusing to address with them as well. I realized that I had never really sat down and told my wife about all of the women that had hurt me in my life and how that hurt was now impacting me in my new surroundings. I don't even think I knew how much it was impacting me. I kept a lot of it inside because I felt that rehashing all of the painful memories of my past somehow dishonored my present. Besides, it was the past! What good would it do to bring it up now? But had I shared this information with her sooner, we likely would have approached our marriage, and our blended family, differently.

Taccara probably would have been more sensitive to my anxiety entering into this environment. We would have had more intentional conversations with our children about what safety and trust means to a new family. We would have included them in our premarital counseling. And we likely would have made more of an effort to foster an environment of trust between us all. But it wasn't too late, and it's not too late for you either.

The Pillar of Trust

The pillar of trust is demonstrated faith in your spouse and exercised faithfulness to your spouse. Each individual in the marriage has the dual responsibility of being trusting as well as trustworthy. If either breaks down, the entire pillar of trust will crumble, leaving the marriage uncovered.

This is the most important pillar of the 4-Pillars because trust must exist in order for the other three to be effective. If trust crumbles, then the other pillars fall. When trust is built, the others are strengthened and aligned.

Implied Trust

The most interesting thing about trust is that it's not something we are taught. We don't learn to build it; we don't even earn it. Trust is simply implied or presumed. When we first meet someone that we are thinking about dating, there is assumed trust even with no pre-existing relationship. By continuing to date them, by opening ourselves up to them, and by endeavoring to share our lives and space with them, it is implied that we trust them. In the beginning of your relationship, how often did you ask your husband or wife, "Do you trust me?" Most of us didn't. It was just there.

Even the standard marriage vows don't include a line that asks you to promise to trust or be trustworthy:

"I [your name] take you [your spouse's name] to be my [wife, husband]
To have and to hold from this day forward
For better, for worse
For richer, for poorer
In sickness and in health
To love and to cherish
Till death do us part…"

The vows include receiving each other in almost all conditions and circumstances for a lifetime. They even include the promise to love. Love? Shouldn't that be implied as well? Sure, but as we all know, emotional love can be fickle, but intentional love takes effort. So, even marriage vows require a promise to love while trust is the characteristic that is implied. It is the unspoken binder of any vow, promise, or contract. No one gets to the table or down the aisle without trust.

Trust is either established, built, or rebuilt through action. We prove that we are trustworthy to one another through consistent actions. From merely keeping our word to following through on our responsibilities to even taking care of each other's needs, the presence of trust produces safety, which leads to security. No marriage is able to flourish without these.

Before realizing that we were walking around with hidden distrust, Taccara and I had a consistent "space" between us that we were afraid to infiltrate. It was "trust" with protective gear. The only thing that was going to break through these walls of distrust was our willingness to become everything that neither of us had ever fully had before. Trust in action wasn't a matter of proving; it was a matter of being.

The Two Sides of Trust

There are two sides to trust: trustworthy and trust-willing. As husband and wife, both are necessary to maintain a covering over your spouse. You carry the responsibility of demonstrating both sides to your spouse at any given moment. In the economy of your marriage, trustworthiness and trust-willingness is a two-sided coin that are dually valuable in your marriage.

Trust-Willing:
Demonstrated Faith in Your Spouse

In the Bible, the word "faith" has several different meanings. One meaning is a belief system, as in a person being of a particular faith. Another meaning of "faith" is to have a demonstrated trust in something or someone. That latter meaning is identical to what we call *trust-willing*.

Trust-willingness is more than the willingness to trust in your spouse; it is the intended effort to show that you trust in your spouse or have faith in your spouse. It isn't just believing them; it's welcoming and allowing your spouse to be depended upon. It's your show of confidence in your spouse's faithfulness in all things. Trust-willingness is inviting your spouse to cover you while submitting yourself to being covered.

"And without faith it is impossible to please him, for whoever would draw near to God must believe that he exists and that he rewards those who seek him." **Hebrews 11:6 ESV**

Without trust in God, it's not only impossible to please Him, it repels Him. The inability to trust God creates a distance between you and Him, but when you exercise trust, you are "drawing near" to God. You become dependent and reliant on Him, and you close the distance between you and Him. When you consider the fact that the Bible is a book about God's relationship to us (His church), then this Scripture is showing us what is required for us to please and grow closer in our relationship with God. If this applies to our relationship with God, then that same principle should also exist in our relationship with one another.

Without trust, it is impossible to connect with your spouse. When you attempt to exist without trust, you repel each other and push each other away. When you operate in trust, it brings you closer together.

"Now faith is confidence in what we hope for and assurance about what we do not see." **Hebrews 11:1 NIV**

While the verse is about faith or trust-willingness in God, the same principles apply to your trust-willingness in marriage. Trust-willingness in your spouse produces in you an expectation of their promises while you wait to receive them in full confidence. It pleases your spouse and gives them a sense of pride when they can experience your show of anticipation to receive what is hoped for from them. Now, we know that your spouse is, in fact, not God, so we understand that they will disappoint you sometimes. In order for the occasional disappointment to not taint the stability of trust, however, disappointment cannot ever be habitual. They must be trustworthy.

Trustworthy:
Exercised Faithfulness to Your Spouse

Being *trustworthy* is not simply the ability to be trusted; it's a statement of who you are or a demonstrated character trait. Trustworthiness is a statement that says that if you can be trusted with it, then you are built for it, committed to it, dependable for it, loyal to it, open to it, and consistent regarding it.

When a person has shown that they cannot be trusted, then they have shown that their character is broken. This is not to say that they are irreparable, but if they don't heal or mature and develop a trustworthy character, then they will never be worthy of their spouse's trust.

"If you have not been faithful in that which is another's, who will give you that which is your own?" **Luke 16:12 NIV**

Being a trustworthy spouse gives you two duties. The first is to be a steward of the spouse that has been entrusted to you by God through covenant. The second duty is to treat your spouse not only as if they belong to you, but as if they are a part of you. Your husband or wife is a child of God, as well as your spouse. Being trustworthy to your spouse shows God that you are capable of being trusted with His child's heart. Being trustworthy to your husband or wife is showing them that you are built for them and are deserving of their confidence.

Taccara and I are in a much better place now. We are happy to report that we have developed a system of faith in and faithfulness to one another. In establishing the pillar of trust, especially in our blended family setting, there had to be an "all hands on deck" approach. We didn't simply lock our children away to "do as we say" and not help them understand the changes that were happening to an environment that they had grown accustomed to. We gave them the responsibility of making the environment safe for us, just as we had the responsibility to make it safe for them.

As we grew (and continue to grow) in trust, we exercised patience. We knew that mistakes would happen, but we made the environment safe for everyone to do so. We knew that boundaries would be tested, but we developed a system of security to help everyone understand limits. Through all of this, trust flourished, just as our family did.

Trust vs. Entrusting

Entrusting means to delegate responsibility. It's having something of value in your possession and placing it in the care of someone else. In marriage, entrusting also means being wise enough to take your hands off of something that you refuse to let go of. Entrusting is exercising trust-willingness in an area by recognizing your spouse can handle it.

Just because you do everything well on your own, doesn't mean you should. Marriage is a partnership. This means trusting someone else with responsibilities that you are used to handling on your own. Entrusting means having the confidence in your spouse to handle the things you'd rather control. This is how your marriage flourishes.

My nature is subtle, but I am very headstrong. I love Taccara with all my heart, but there are certain things I'd rather do myself or, if I'm honest, things I'd rather control. Control is a symptom of distrust. Being in business with my wife challenged me to not just trust her, but to entrust her with areas that she is much better equipped to handle than me. I had to trust her ideas, thoughts, and insights in areas that I was not willing to let go of. I had to relinquish control (distrust) and share the space I occupied. In doing so, I found that she was extraordinarily better at some things than I am. I had to then acknowledge where I was weak and entrust my weaker areas to her. Once I recognized that Taccara was a trustworthy asset, it allowed me to be trust-willing enough to receive guidance from her. I demonstrate my trust-willingness in working with her and asking for her help.

Whether it's cooking, cleaning, business, or finances, for the sake of your marriage, learn to just let go. Even if they do things differently than the way you do, let it go. That's how you build a strong partnership within your marriage. When each spouse trusts the other to uphold them and be strong in their areas of weakness, they become the epitome of a power couple.

Trust Exercise & Discussion Questions

1. When you first met your husband or wife, what characteristics did they exhibit that made you trust them?
2. Now that you are married, do you still believe that you exhibit trust-willingness towards your spouse? *If not, explain why. What has happened that has broken down your willingness to trust them?* **Set aside some time to discuss this later.**
3. Does your spouse believe that you are trust-willing? *If you answered no, why do you think they feel this way?*
4. Are you trustworthy? *Why or why not? (This is your chance to either brag on yourself or be completely transparent.)*
5. When you first met your husband or wife, how did you demonstrate trustworthiness to them?
6. Has anything changed from how you demonstrated trustworthiness to them when you first met to how you are today? *If yes, what has changed? Be thoughtful about this, and then be honest with yourself.* **Set aside some time to discuss this later.**
7. Are there any areas in your marriage that your spouse is good at but you refuse to **entrust** the responsibilities to them? *If so, why do you think it's hard to relinquish control in these areas?*

Trust Exercise: After reviewing your answers with your spouse, set aside some time to discuss what can be done to improve the existence of trust-willingness and trustworthiness in your marriage. Rewrite your wedding vows so that you now include your commitment to both in your marriage.

Establishing the Pillar of Trust

The pillar of trust and its two sides speak to marital fidelity and physical and emotional faithfulness to your spouse, but there is so much more. The true value of this pillar is found in day-to-day, moment-to-moment acts of trust.

Functioning in Trust-Willingness

1. Trust your spouse's ability and desire to show up for you.
2. Trust your spouse's desire to provide safety and security for you.
3. Trust your spouse's intentions so that they are safe to make mistakes with you.
4. Trust that your spouse hears you.
5. Trust that your spouse is honest.
6. Trust your spouse with your honesty.
7. Trust that your spouse is open to you.
8. Trust your spouse with your vulnerabilities.

Functioning in Trustworthiness

1. Your spouse must be able to trust that you are honest.
2. Your spouse must be able to trust that you will receive their honesty.
3. Your spouse must be able to trust that you are

dependable.
4. Your spouse must be able to trust that you will keep your word.
5. Your spouse must be able to trust that you have secured the doors of your relationship.
6. Your spouse must be able to trust that they are safe with you.
7. Your spouse must be able to trust that your criticism or correction is not meant to harm but to support and enhance.
8. Your spouse has to know that you're transparent, open, and vulnerable with them.
9. Your spouse must be able to trust you with their vulnerabilities.

When you look at the above list, know that both trust-willingness and trustworthiness apply to you. It's not going to be easy, especially if you don't trust your spouse in certain areas. It's even harder if you've broken trust in particularly hurtful ways. It can be equally as hard for newlyweds who are learning how to live with each other while at the same time letting go of their independent lives. Nevertheless, both instances of trust apply to each spouse. You must build this pillar daily and consistently. You have to consciously practice asking yourself, "Was that trustworthy of me?" or "Am I trusting them in this area?" Practice both sides of the pillar of trust at one time to build or rebuild this pillar in your marriage.

Empathy

Remember that first big fight that I told you Kenyon and I had? While it would be ideal to tell you that we learned everything we needed to from that experience and never fought again, that's simply not true. We've had several fights after that, but each time we have fought, we actually learned something different about ourselves and our marriage. Just before deciding to write this book, we had one of our biggest and most transformational fights yet.

It was my daughter's sweet-16 birthday party and we had rented a party bus for her and her friends to take to an escape room. Kenyon and I were on the bus as well, and everyone was having a blast. I was dancing and singing (LOUDLY) and Kenyon just shook his head in equal parts amusement and despair. On the way home, though, something changed. Have you ever had one of those moments when you notice that something shifts within your spouse and their mood suddenly changes? I had no idea what had just happened, and by the time we'd made it back home, we were in full-on fight mode... via text.

Kenyon: What is your problem?
Me: Are you kidding me? YOU'RE the one that just suddenly shut down with an attitude!
Kenyon: You just shut the door in my face. That's so disrespectful.
Me: I didn't even realize you were behind me. I was distracted.
Kenyon: So now I'm invisible, huh? You knew I was there, you just didn't care. That's how you get.
Me: Oh, come ON! You know good and well that's not what I meant. Stop playing the victim. You're upset at me and I didn't

even do anything!
Kenyon: Oh, so because I have feelings and I'm frustrated, I'm playing the victim? I can't ever say anything about my feelings without you doing this. You always get defensive and dismiss my feelings!
Me: Just because I disagree with what you're saying doesn't mean I'm being dismissive, Kenyon!
...

This went on for 24 hours. For a full day, we were going back and forth like this, refusing to see where the other was coming from, and choosing which angry word to hang on to at each juncture. If Kenyon said I "always" did something, I saw his "always" and raised him a "never." If I threw an insensitive insult at him, he threw a fighting word right back at me. By the end of the next day, I was dazed and crying out of sheer frustration and confusion. To add insult to injury, Kenyon had the nerve to text me saying that I needed to pray and listen to some worship to pull myself out of the mood I was in. "Listen to worship?" I said. "Are you freaking kidding me? I am spent over everything that just happened yesterday and your only response at this moment is that I pray and listen to worship?"

"Well...yeah," he said, and just like that, another fight ensued... via text.

I didn't feel insulted because he'd asked me to pray or listen to worship. I'm not a heathen. Knowing that I suffer from anxiety and could over-do it when I was this upset, he probably knew that I needed to find a way to channel what I was feeling. But that's not how it came across to me at that moment. I felt insulted because it seemed as if he was using this as a way to avoid hearing me or apologizing to me. I felt wronged and it seemed like he was using our faith to fake our way through everything that had been said and done. I had zero desire to listen to worship, but I did pray. "God, make him see what he did wrong! Make him apologize! God, don't let him rest until he gets it! Amen."

Finally, we sat down and decided to try to talk it through face to face. By the end of the conversation, I was grateful for this fight. After shouting back and forth for what felt like hours and disagreeing over who had said what, we realized that we had actual transcripts of the fight! Now I could prove how right I was because it was all documented! So, we went to the very top of where it all began in our text messages.

"See, when you said this, it made me feel anxious and nervous because I didn't understand where it was coming from," I said.

"Well, I'm sorry it came across like that. What made me say that was...because I felt..." Kenyon replied.

For two hours, we sat and dissected every message, every sentence, and every word that was typed. The conversation went from trying to prove a point and being right to seeing each other and what was lost in translation. We had literally been having two completely different fights. And since we weren't talking to each other, our fights escalated based on the stories we were telling ourselves about what the other was saying. Once we figured this out, we allowed each other to communicate what we actually meant. We left room in our hearts and minds to hear what the other was saying and to feel what they felt. We locked ourselves in our bedroom and refused to leave until we understood each other. By the time we were ready to leave that room, I knew that I had some apologizing to do.

The Pillar of Empathy

Empathy is the desire and ability to hear, feel, and understand your spouse. It gives voice to their emotions and makes their experiences matter. The presence of empathy in your marriage improves communication, strengthens your intimate connection, and stabilizes your emotions in conflict.

I love my husband—I love him with everything that I am—but I would be doing our marriage a disservice if I believed that loving him or telling him that I love him is all that he needs from me. While reading a book by psychotherapist Lori Gottlieb, I read that the most romantic thing you can ever say to your spouse is not "I love you," it's "I understand you." Kenyon and I couldn't agree more. Being married is more than just committing to being there and never leaving. It's committing to never giving up in the constant pursuit of learning each other. It's searching for new ways to see and understand each other. It's never taking for granted who our spouse is today and who they are becoming.

When couples tell us that they are considering divorce because they've "fallen out of love," it's one of the most heartbreaking things to hear. We say this because if this truly is the only reason for considering divorce, it likely could have been prevented long before the marriage reached this point. Couples don't just fall out of love. They don't mysteriously end up on the steps of the divorce courthouse from events they "never saw coming." They saw what was coming. They just didn't recognize the signs. Life happened or children came, and, without a thought, predictability set in.

Once a spouse becomes predictable, it's easy to set the marriage on autopilot and allow habits to steer the direction of the relationship. It becomes painfully difficult to demonstrate empathy in your marriage once you've decided that you know everything there is to know about your spouse's wants, desires, and feelings.

In this chapter, we are going to explore three areas in your marriage that rely heavily on your ability to exercise empathy towards your spouse: communication, conflict, and connection. Within these three areas, you will find many of the missing pieces of your marriage that you thought had faded with the "honeymoon" phase of your relationship—the pieces that would have you believe that your marriage is dying or that you're falling out of love with each other. Your marriage isn't dead. It's sleeping, even if it is comatose. Don't you think it's time to wake it up?

Empathy in Communication

Kenyon's mother, Sherri, is one of the strongest and toughest women I have ever met. Since I care for my mother, I think I instantly connected with Sherri because I watched her care for her mother until her mother passed. She did it with such dignity and grace. However, that wasn't the relationship that impressed me the most. More than 30 years after her senior prom, she married her prom date. It was the most romantic thing I'd ever heard of. Years after living separate lives, raising their children, and even experiencing heartache, they found one another. Even though a stroke had left Walter (Walt) without the ability to speak anymore, he still found the words to ask her to marry him. And even though Walt had a physical handicap, they never let it handicap their relationship.

I cannot begin to imagine what it would feel like to suddenly wake up and not be able to utter the words that I can hear in my head so clearly. Beyond not being able to hold simple conversations, I would go crazy not being able to communicate my wants or needs. But I don't see Walt going crazy. Sherri gave him his voice back. Not that it isn't difficult or frustrating for him, but I believe what helps him is her desire to understand him, even if no one else does.

I see how she speaks to him and, when the situation calls for it, speaks for him. While it would be so easy for her to simply give him what she wants him to have or what she thinks he needs,

I've watched her search him for his words. She listens to him through his eyes, touch, mood shifts, and non-verbal cues. She waits for him to tell her what he wants in his time and in his own way.

It would take an immense amount of patience and empathy to be able to communicate with your spouse when they can't speak a word to you. While the average couple can hear and speak to each other with no limitations, it's easy to become indifferent about communication with your spouse because you've stopped searching them for understanding. Good communication is a simple gesture of searching their mood, tone, or rhythms for a deeper understanding of where they are (mentally or emotionally). Empathy in communication forces you to repeatedly abandon assumptions and familiarity so that you can find your spouse. This is best achieved through asking questions.

Asking Questions Is an Act of Empathy in Communication

My mind goes a million miles a minute. When Kenyon's mood changes or shifts, I try to stop and ask, "Okay, what just happened? What did I miss?" In this way, I can quickly check his temperature and control mine. If he comes to me with anything that instantly pricks me or "rubs me the wrong way," I take deep breaths and ask questions so I don't make assumptions. "Just so I'm clear, are you saying...?" This one question has stopped many fights in our home. Not only is it a great use of active listening (re-stating what he said back to him), it also forces me to turn "auto-pilot" off and engage with my spouse as opposed to reacting to him.

Kenyon does the same for me. When he can feel that my mood or my rhythm is off, he will ask the typical question, "Are you okay?" And he's genuinely asking. What we do not do in these moments is lie to each other. We don't passive-aggressively say, "I'm fine," or, "Nothing's wrong," when it's obvious that something is. We share when we're upset (whether it's with each other or something else). We respond honestly to our spouse's attempts to "feel" where we are in sensitive moments so that we can develop healthy habits of navigating each other during these times. We give each other time alone if we can feel that they need space. We let each other know when we're not okay but don't want to talk about it. And finally, we try not to allow our offense to dictate how we respond to each other in these moments. We give each other what we need, and, if needed, we provide space to address it later.

Yes, communication is more than just asking questions when something is wrong, but it's often when on the verge of a breakdown that your weakness in communication is apparent. The practice of asking each other questions to "search" for one another has become easy for us because we continue to do this even when things are going well. When the boat is not being rocked, it's easy to miss the waves that are an indicator of the turbulence ahead. So, we've made it a priority to ask each other questions, especially when things are good between us. In this way, the idea of asking questions is not something foreign or something that we only do when we're trying to get to the bottom of something.

Work at finding ways to communicate throughout the day. Kenyon sends simple messages in the middle of the day to ask, "You good, babe?" which is his way of asking how my day is going. It's a simple invitation to share my world with him, and it's his way of searching me for my words.

It is necessary to let your partner know that they are safe to approach you and ask questions and that they can trust you to be honest with them about "where you are." They are showing empathy by trying to connect with you. By acknowledging their attempt and actually trying to communicate and help them understand where you are, you are demonstrating empathy towards them. When you reject their attempts to communicate with you or passive-aggressively respond to their attempts, they will eventually stop trying to "search" for you.

Empathy in Communication Exercise

1. Do you believe your spouse (their desires, their actions, or their conversation) is predictable? If so, how?
2. If you answered yes to the first question, do you think believing that your spouse is predictable has caused you to believe that you no longer need to search them for understanding?
3. Imagine that your spouse was unable to speak. Are you confident in your ability to be able to search them for their needs and desires?
4. Do you think asking questions in your conversations could help the communication in your marriage?

Empathy in Communication Exercise Continued

5. When your spouse comes to you and asks, "Are you okay?" or "What's wrong?" do you respond honestly (in love) or do you reject their attempts to communicate with you? If you don't respond honestly, why not? *If the answer is that they haven't received your responses well in the past, be honest and discuss this later. Perhaps there is something that you both could be doing to make these conversations more loving and empathetic towards one another.*
6. For one week, create opportunities to communicate with one another throughout the day.

    a. Jot down some ideas of how you can attempt to communicate: *Ask them how their day is going; ask them if they need anything before you head home from work; ask if you can do anything to make their day or week better; ask if you can help with anything around the house this week; ask them how they slept; get the idea?*

    b. Get out your cell phone and program your alarm to set reminders of what to do (if you have an iPhone, you can label your alarms to remind you of the communication attempt). Using your calendar works as well.

    c. At the end of the week (on a Sunday), set aside some time to discuss how this exercise made you feel.

Empathy in Conflict

In the *Empathy in Communication* section, we suggested asking questions before reacting to your spouse. This will be especially challenging if your marriage is in a season of consistent conflict. Conflict trains you to be on constant guard, waiting for an attack, and armed with some form of retaliation. Being in a constant place of reaction or retaliation removes your ability to hear each other. It's often not until reckless damage has been done that you will realize that you two are no longer fighting over the issue that started it all, but instead you're fighting to be heard. Remember, Kenyon and I spent an entire day fighting two completely different fights because we refused to take the time to hear each other. What a difference a simple question would have made for us. Imagine what stopping in the moment and asking a simple question can do for your marriage in conflict.

Frustration will come. It is guaranteed that your spouse will do things that will challenge your patience. Empathy in conflict filters your frustrations and your words through love first. Before exploding, it forces you to ask the question, *"How can I communicate this to my husband or wife in a way that helps them understand me and doesn't damage them in the process?"* Erupting with emotion will only serve you in that moment. Choosing empathy in those moments will serve your marriage for a lifetime.

The same can be said for being on the receiving end of your spouse's frustrations. When your spouse brings you their frustrations using empathy, they've likely wrestled with exactly how and when to communicate this to you in the most loving way possible. They love you. They see the best in you. They never want you to feel like you're not good enough. But they also understand that, in order for you both to grow together, there will always be things that have to be addressed. Becoming defensive or allowing your emotions to react before giving your heart time to respond immediately devalues your spouse's need to be heard. When you become defensive and challenge their empathy with hostility, you stunt your marriage's ability to mature and grow.

Managing conflict has less to do with what happens in the fight than what happens before it all begins. Your assumptions about your spouse's disposition, your tone in your approach, or even your body language can have either a positive or negative impact on how conflict is resolved, or whether or not it is resolved at all. The goal is not to try to discourage or avoid conflict. We want you to use empathy to help minimize the probability of the conflict erupting into something unnecessary or unmanageable.

Here Are Five Keys for Demonstrating Empathy in Conflict:

1. **Remember that your spouse is your brother or sister in Christ first** — This is an important distinction because it helps you to not take their familiarity for granted. When you go to church, when you are surrounded by friends in faith, you are always aware of how you speak and respond to them. You position your tone so you don't

hurt them. You are considerate of their struggles, so you don't necessarily hold their bad days against them. And, hopefully, you filter your words through love so that you are always showing them the love of Jesus first.

When you approach and receive your spouse with this same posture first, it literally tempers how you interact with them and react to them at all times.

2. **Respond to conflict with the end in mind** — This may seem very "fluffy" or airy, but it's something to consider. How do you want your thoughts and feelings to be between you and your spouse when all is said and done? When you consider the end first, it should cause you to choose your approach and responses more wisely.

3. **Ask questions first, respond later** — Develop the habit of not making assumptions. Seek to understand. Seek clarity. Then seek to be understood.

4. **If it matters to your spouse, it should matter to you** — So many conflicts begin or become persistent because one spouse believes the subject at hand is "no big deal." Not only does this invalidate your spouse's feelings, it makes them feel as if you don't care about what hurts them. If you are truly on a mission to become one, then you must adopt a holistic mindset of "what's yours is mine and what's mine is yours." This does not only address material things, it should also address their cares, their hurts, and their burdens.

If your spouse brings you an issue that is hurting them, it's important to respond to their issue with empathy. *"Where does it hurt? Why does it hurt? What can I (or we) do to help make it stop hurting?"* Even if it is something that wouldn't necessarily bother you, what can keep your marriage growing is your ability to respond to their hurt as if it were your own.

5. ***Commit to hearing each other, not being right*** — One of the most damaging places we can get to while in conflict is the place where we become deaf to what our spouse is truly saying simply because we need to be right. If you go into conversations of conflict with the purpose of being right, you automatically make them an enemy. When you commit to hearing them, you're committing to making them, their feelings, and their experiences matter. You're committing to understanding them above all else.

Conflict is Reflective

Our spouse is a reflection of both who we are to them and how we treat them. Sometimes, we fiercely protest the demonstration of empathy because it forces us to look at our "reflection" honestly. If we haven't been safe or secure for them, or if we've disregarded their needs, then perhaps the negative feelings they have, or the negative responses they exhibit towards us, is a direct reflection of who we have been to them.

This is not to say this is always the case. Some spouses do use deflection as a manipulative tool to make you believe that how they are acting is your fault. We're not saying that you should respond to deflection attempts. But let's be real: You know if or when you haven't been the best partner to your spouse or if you haven't treated them right. What we want you to recognize is that emotions in conflict will always reflect what happened before the conflict began. It exposes true feelings and unearths deficits in your marriage that have been ignored over time. Empathy in conflict helps you see beyond their emotions so that you can search them to understand not just where they are (mentally or emotionally), but why they are there. It doesn't always feel good, but it is necessary.

This level of empathy in conflict requires vulnerability. It requires both of you to be willing to be seen by each other. It removes the layer of selfishness and reveals all insecurities. When your spouse brings you their grievances, it means they've discovered that you're not perfect. When you share your grievances with your spouse, you may be afraid that they will shut down and reject you for "exposing" their imperfections. So, this level of empathy requires safety so that you can be vulnerable with them, security so that your insecurities are guarded by them, and trust that they won't hold your vulnerability against you.

Empathy in Conflict Exercise & Discussion Questions

1. Do you believe that asking simple questions in conflict can avoid misunderstandings in your marriage? *I.e. "Explain what you mean by that..." "Let me make sure I understand you...are you saying...?"*
2. How often do the conflicts in your marriage become more about being right than understanding each other? If it happens often, why do you think you take such a defensive posture towards one another?
3. Which one of the Five Keys for *Demonstrating Empathy* in Conflict is the most important for you in your marriage? Which do you wish your spouse practiced more of?
4. If conflicts in your marriage reflect how you treat your spouse, what would your "reflection" through your spouse reveal about you?
5. What does your spouse's "reflection" in conflict reveal about them? Write it down and then pick a time later to discuss this.

Empathy in Connection

Marriages today, on a cellular level, are made up of both significant and insignificant connections. How we greet each other, how we reach for one another (literally or figuratively), or even how we ignore one another are all points of connection that we have with our spouse on a daily basis. Empathy in connection is the ability to demonstrate an intuitive awareness or mindfulness of our spouse. Every day, through both large and small gestures, your spouse is asking you, "Are you here for me?" And every day, your actions, reactions, or non-actions are communicating to them either yes or no. It's a persistent demonstration of awareness and acknowledgement.

Kenyon and I work from home together. He is usually in the basement studio and I am in the office on the main floor. You would think that it would be difficult for us to work together in the same house every day, but it's not. We get extremely busy with meetings, client calls, taking and picking up kids to and from school, etc. and there will be days that we barely connect. I am typically okay without speaking until bedtime, where we can connect and download about our days. Kenyon, on the other hand, requires a different type of connection during or throughout the day to let him know that "I'm here." There will be some days when I will send a random text, saying, "Hey babe, I miss you." On other days, I will walk to his workspace just to give him a kiss on the cheek.
"What was that for?" he'll usually ask.

"Just cause I love you," I'll say. And I'll walk away. I don't do things like this to patronize him or to coddle his insecurities. It's my sincere desire to let him know that I acknowledge what he needs to feel connected to me, and, because I love him, I am happy to oblige.

Dr. Carl Rogers defines empathy as being able to discern the internal frame of a person. It's having a moment-by-moment sensitivity to the needs and desires of each other. I have to remain constantly in tune with myself and conscientiously aware of my husband's needs in order for this to become a part of the fabric of our marriage. What's interesting is, we've never really sat down and asked each other, "What do you need in order to feel connected to me?" We've become intuitively aware of one another first through demonstration, then through conflict.

Since most people will begin a relationship demonstrating love in their own "language," I paid attention to how Kenyon began connecting with me early in our relationship. How he communicated with me, how he wanted to spend time with me, and even how he exhibited affection towards me were all reflective manifestations of what he needed and desired from me. If I had remained unaware of what he was communicating to me and only loved in my own language, there is a strong possibility that Kenyon and I would be constantly feeling disconnected in our marriage.

The second way we became intuitively aware of one another was in conflict. When we came to each other with frustrations of how we were spoken to or perhaps the way we were treated in certain instances, we stored each other's feelings into our memories and our hearts to constantly remind us of when we could be causing potential damage to our spouse. Empathy in connection automatically creates compassion for your spouse. By empathizing with their hurt in conflict, even when it's uncomfortable to you, you make way for the compassion that will want to do whatever it takes to not only stop their hurting, but to ensure that they never hurt again.

We had dinner with our friends Jacob and Mari to celebrate Mari's birthday. Somehow, we got on the subject of whether or not Mari got what she wanted for her birthday, and she quickly blurted out, "No I did NOT!" Jacob was stunned because, in Jacob-fashion, he had surprised her with a car. A nice car. Mari saying that she didn't get what she wanted felt like a slap in the face.

"Don't get me wrong," Mari said, "it's a nice car and very upscale. But I asked for a car that wouldn't be too expensive to maintain so that we could save more money. And that's not even what I wanted for my birthday. I wanted to get a sitter, go to a concert"—her favorite artist was in town—"and then spend a quiet evening in bed watching movies." Mari felt that if she couldn't get the car she wanted, she should have at least gotten one of the gifts she asked for, even if it was just time with Jacob in bed.

This exchange was not at all surprising to Kenyon and me. We had heard a version of this argument every year. Mari wants to take more vacations together and spend more time with Jacob. Jacob wants to be home and work on his car hobby. Jacob likes quiet dinners at home and can't understand why "sex-on-demand" isn't a thing when he buys Mari a car. Mari simply wants more connection outside the bedroom to stimulate her desire for sex. Jacob and Mari fell in love with each other without ever becoming fully aware of each other. You would think they didn't really know each other at all, but they knew each other for 12 years before getting married. Or did they?

When we ask couples to demonstrate this level of empathy in connection, many feel like we are asking them to change who they are. And, in some ways, we are, but changing who they are isn't something that hasn't already begun to happen. Did you know that your brain's neural networks are naturally designed to change in order to accommodate the presence of your husband or wife? You have changed. That doesn't change your individuality, but it does add to you a mental and emotional placeholder for your spouse's presence in your life. Your spouse becomes your habit. Now your behaviors towards your spouse are habits too; they are based upon your level of awareness of your spouse. We aren't asking anyone to change; we are asking them to change their minds about their husband or wife. We are suggesting that they start considering their spouse's needs, desires, and importance. We are asking couples to be more aware of their husband or wife which will in turn change their behavior towards them. Over time, that new behavior becomes a natural inclination, a new habit. When you get down to where the rubber meets the road, what we are really telling couples to do is to stop fighting against how God has already designed their brain for marriage—to be more aware and attuned to their spouses in their everyday life.

Considering this, let's revisit the notion of "falling out of love." When you are consciously aware of each other in your marriage, it becomes more difficult to simply fall out of love. You begin to sense when your partner's rhythm is off. You master the art of searching for each other so that you can always uncover ways to get back "in step" with one another. You begin to sense and see the road to "falling out of love" in enough time to course-correct because you'll know that the moment you stop connecting is the moment you begin to fall apart.

Perhaps connecting to your spouse isn't about quirky text messages or phone calls. Maybe they want to be able to share more about their work with you. Maybe they want you to respond to them when they send articles that they find interesting. Perhaps they desire to have more meaningful conversations with you. Maybe they literally want you to ask, "Do you feel connected to me?" The beauty and the barrier to empathy in connection is all about becoming aware of and acknowledging what your spouse desires and needs from you.

If this is hard for you, if it is challenging to open yourself to develop, cultivate, or demonstrate empathy in connection, consider that this may be due to a pillar having been breached or broken along the way. And while it could be plain stubbornness, we would love to believe that no one would ever intentionally withhold empathy from their spouse in this way.

In the final chapter of this book, we are going to address the steps that a couple must take to repair the broken pillars in their marriage.

Empathy in Connection Exercise & Discussion Questions

1. On a scale of 1-10, how would you rate your level of awareness of your spouse? 1 being not very aware, 10 being acutely aware.
2. On a scale of 1-10, how would you rate your spouse's level of awareness of you? 1 being not very aware, 10 being acutely aware. Pick a time to discuss your answer here.
3. **Empathy in Connection Activity Part 1:** First, think of all of the ways you desire to connect with your spouse. What do you want from them? What do you miss about how you used to connect? Write these down.

    a. hen, for three days, do all of those things for your spouse. POUR IT ON!

    b. For each spouse: Your job is to turn on your awareness to your spouse's gestures and attempts to connect with you. What are you learning from them? Keep a list. This is teaching you how to discern your spouse's love language.

    c. At the end of the three days, sit down and tell your spouse how they desire to be connected to based on what you observed in their behavior.

4. **Empathy in Connection Activity Part 2:** Now that you understand what your spouse needs in order to feel connected to you, for the next three days, practice connecting to them in the way they desire. Hint: You've now got an entire list of ideas.

Establishing the Pillar of Empathy

Here are four rules to live by when establishing the pillar of empathy in your marriage:

1. *Never lose sight of them* — Times will get hard and days will get busy. But the road to falling out of love is paved with assumptions of who your spouse is. Find them every day and discover something new.

2. *Never stop pursuing oneness* — Becoming one is about more than merging your lives. It's about becoming fluent in your spouse's rhythm.

3. *Always be sensitive to each other's needs* — Learn to treat their needs and desires as your own. Your spouse is a part of you.

4. *Always ask questions* — Before you get offended. Before you get upset. Before you allow your thoughts to deceive you about what your spouse is thinking, ask questions to clarify where they are coming from.

5. *Never forget to look them in the eye and affirm how they feel* — They should always know that their feelings and their experiences matter to you.

Repairing Broken Pillars

In Case of Emergency

Intimacy is one of the most beautiful and terrifying places a person can choose to be. On one hand, you have the comfort, assurance, and life that true intimacy and closeness brings. On the other hand, you have the very real fact that another person holds your heart and the deepest places of you in their hands, with the ability to crush your world at any given moment. The truth: No matter how much you love someone, or how much they love you, hurt is an inevitable part of intimacy. While there will be varying degrees to the hurt that is caused, there is almost always a path back to oneness and true intimacy.

Repairing broken pillars is all about preparing you for the inevitable hurt that every marriage will experience, regardless of how catastrophic or inconsequential that hurt is. In this chapter, we felt it was important for us to address the "for worse" portion of the "for better or worse" statement in your vows. It is easy to only focus on the good and encourage you in good times, but we wanted to give a guide to finding your way back to each other when things are shaky. So, in case of emergency, this is for you.

Perpetual mistakes deteriorate your ability to cover your spouse by breaking down the 4-Pillars that you just learned about. When the pillars fall, emotional walls are built because your spouse will feel like they have to protect themselves. Some walls will be mere fences while others will be fortresses. Regardless of the size, emotional walls create barriers to loving each other. Your marriage will not survive if one or both of you insists on living within the walls that you've created for yourselves. Repairing broken pillars will help tear down these walls, renew your covering, and recover your marriage.

In this chapter, we're going to show you how the pillars work together to reestablish your covering. We'll help you understand what gets broken when hurt or disappointment occurs, and the order in which each pillar should be rebuilt. We'll take you step-by-step from the point of feeling helpless about the current state of your marriage to feeling hopeful for the future of your marriage.

Rules of Engagement During Periods of Repair

1. The road and process to repair won't be easy. Be okay with it being hard, so you don't try to take shortcuts and make the process something it wasn't designed to be.

2. Your marriage is made of two people, and it required you both to get here. The rebuilding of your marriage will require you both as participants as well. No one person can do it alone. You must work together to remain together.

3. Change will not happen overnight, so you will have to be patient with yourselves and each other while also being

diligent and consistent. When you feel like you want to give up, remember this fact and keep going.

4. There will come times when you will want to monitor each other's efforts, progress, or responses, but try to resist. Otherwise, you risk restricting your own progress.

5. You are going to want to measure your "cooperation" in the repair process by their level of cooperation and participation. Don't use them as an excuse to do or not do the right thing. Do the right thing because it's right.

Our goal for this chapter will not be to repair or solve every problem in every marriage. The goal is to help repair who you are when problems arise in your marriage. We want to show you how to repair your thoughts about your spouse in times that you don't even want to see them. Finally, we want to repair how you treat your spouse when they've crossed a line, even when you feel like they deserve the worst of you. If you've injured your spouse, we want to help you learn the mindset and steps needed to repair the harm caused. Who you are consistently, and where you are emotionally in every issue of repair is vital to recovering your marriage and your spouse.

The Transgressor and the Claimant

In every situation where there has been a breach of contract or, in our case, a broken pillar, there is a *transgressor* and a *claimant*. We will be using these two terms throughout this chapter, so it's important that we help you understand why before moving forward. The Biblical Hebrew meaning of *transgressor* is someone within a relationship that has broken a trust. Since we have all been the transgressor in our marriage at one time or another, it's important that you don't get hung up on the title. We use the Biblical meaning because we understand that the transgressor didn't just break the trust of their spouse, they also broke their promise to God, the Father of their spouse.

Claimant is a simple term which refers to the person making the claim of being hurt or transgressed against. We will use the title claimant with a dual meaning. First, there's the meaning in the legal sense—someone who sues for damages. The purpose of using it in a legal sense is not to punish the transgressor, but to create a forum for them to acknowledge the damage that has been done. The second meaning we will use *claimant* for is to collect or claim something that they have a right to. Like a beneficiary of a settlement agreement, the claimant has the right to certain benefits of their spouse when a transgression has occurred. That benefit is the covering or recovering. *However*, the claimant can only obtain that benefit if they maintain their commitment to their marriage.

Disclaimer

Every hurt that we feel is real. What's extremely important to understand is that some hurt will be a result of something done to you by your spouse, but there may also be pre-existing areas within you that will cause you to react to perceived hurt.

This does not mean your pain is not real; we just want you to leave room for the possibility that your offense may be misleading you by directing you to the wrong source of your hurt. Be slow to anger and quick to self-evaluate.

reCovering Your Marriage

When we fail, regardless of how or the degree to which we fail, every pillar is affected. However, the epicenter of our marital issue always begins with one specific pillar. When this one pillar is broken, all of the other pillars are then impacted. That pillar is *trust*.

Trust is one pillar that, if broken, shatters all the others. Regardless of what the presenting issue is, as soon as the claimant is impacted by the damage, trust is immediately withdrawn from the transgressor and the marriage as a whole. The claimant (or spouse) is effectively uncovered, as is the transgressor. In order to recover your marriage, it will take a concerted effort to repair all *4-Pillars*. We've designed this process to work with almost any situation that your marriage faces.

Step One of Repair: Empathy

When trying to repair the broken pillars in your marriage, it's easy for both spouses to overlook each other because they are only considering the circumstances from their own point of reference. Empathy in brokenness puts the transgressor in the place of their spouse's pain. It gives their spouse (the claimant) permission to feel that pain while observing the transgressor's attempt to connect with them.

Empathy in connection is the ability to demonstrate intuitive awareness of your spouse, or perceive how they are being affected. Repairing broken pillars will require you to put yourself in the place of your spouse's pain, understand how they are being impacted, and then identifying what is needed to help them heal. You will have to go from a place of simply being told "where it hurts," to a place of anticipating their hurt.

They will feel betrayed. They will feel unworthy. They will feel unlovable. They will feel damaged. They will feel like they aren't and never will be enough. They will feel taken advantage of. They will feel overlooked. They will feel insignificant. They will feel invisible. You will not only have to allow them to feel these things, you will have to sit with them through it all.

To the Claimant: The last thing you will want to do right now is empathize with the transgressor, but if you're going to be here, if you're going to try to repair these pillars, it will require you to connect with them also. We're not suggesting that you accept excuses for their behavior. We're not saying that you should even participate in activities that you aren't comfortable with. We are simply encouraging you to be open to their authentic feelings of remorse and their genuine desire to seek healing. The operative words here are authentic and genuine. If authenticity and genuineness are not present, you will be able to tell, and this process of repair will not be successful.

To the Transgressor: At this juncture, the only thing your spouse feels is pain. There is nothing else for them to feel right now. Yes, they love you, but that love is being challenged by what they currently feel and what they are thinking. Your role at this stage of repair is to connect through their pain. You will want to say, "I'm sorry," wait in the shadows until your spouse has "gotten over it," and then come out of hiding once it's safe to rejoin your marriage. This passive approach will not repair broken pillars, and it will not restore your marriage.

The Transgressor's Responsibility in Empathy Will Be To:

1. ***Observe and Acknowledge the Damage Caused.*** It's important for you to not just admit what has been done, but to own your mistake with no excuses. It doesn't matter what the events or circumstances were that preceded your making this mistake. Anything that deviates from your willingness to take ownership and accountability will appear defensive and disingenuous to your spouse. It doesn't mean that preceding factors aren't important or relevant. However, the most pressing problem is the very real fact that your marriage is here because of your most recent mistake. This must be resolved before anything else is addressed.

2. ***Recognize Why It Was Wrong and Understand Why It Is Painful.*** No matter how big or small the mistake was, your spouse's heart needs to know two things up front: *"Do you know why it was wrong?"* and *"Do you understand how*

much this hurt them?" By being able to clearly define why something was wrong and identify with how much it hurt your spouse, you give them (the claimant) hope in the fact that you possess what it takes to exercise good judgement and rise to the type of character that deserves another chance. Your awareness of their hurt says, "How you feel is important to me."

3. **Demonstrate Authentic Penitence for the Damage Caused.** Penitence is a formal word often used in describing the heart of a believer. To make it simple, it's a personally broken heart for something wrong that you've done. Penitence is authentic remorse and sorrow. This is not to be confused with the pain you feel simply from the embarrassment of being caught. This is the sincere expression and deep sorrow for causing pain to your spouse.

To the Claimant: In being open to their desire to demonstrate authentic remorse for the pain that they have caused, we want to ask you for something seemingly impossible: understanding. We are asking you to be understanding that the transgressor is currently suffering in their own form of hell as well. While the word penitentiary (prison) is a closely related word to penitence, imprisoning your spouse through any form of emotional, verbal, or physical punishment will not help matters in your marriage. You have every right to express your hurt. It is expected that you will take some time to get over this issue. All we are asking is that you not seek to punish the transgressor by making them have to continue to prove that they are sorry. The claimant shares the responsibility of rebuilding, but being a warden is not part of it.

4. **Demonstrate Repentance.** The word repent in the Bible doesn't actually mean to turn away like most of us have been taught. The Hebrew word means to bare blame and make reconciliation, while the Greek word means to change one's mind afterwards. The whole process under the pillar of empathy is one of repentance, but that repentance isn't complete until the transgressor changes their mind after all is said and done.

   Changing your mind is to think differently—to think differently about your spouse, your position as a husband or wife, and the choice(s) you've made. In short, it means you are retreating from thoughts and behaviors that led you here and turning towards a path that compels you to treat your spouse with more value and deep consideration. You will have to be the husband or wife that was promised and make your marriage a priority. Repentance isn't simply stated. It is declared and then acted upon. It assumes that something has demonstrably changed within the transgressor. Whether your transgression was a result of something done or things you've said, this is where your comprehension of what was done and how it hurts your spouse meets your action of doing something different moving forward. In order for change to be received, it must be demonstrated repeatedly over time.

5. **Exercise Long-Term Patience.** The most important thing

for both the claimant and the transgressor to remember in these moments is that emotions are the first to arrive in a relationship, and the last to leave in trauma. Emotions don't change right away, even when people do. Emotions—psychologically, biologically, and intimately—affirm an experience. Even though the transgressor may change, the claimant will still hurt from the past experience. Patience in empathy helps the transgressor to anticipate the need for additional time for the claimant's emotions to catch up with the transgressor's actions. When both the transgressor and the claimant commit to patience, they are committing to having the compassion to wait for each other. The transgressor is awaiting the claimant's full healing. The claimant is waiting for the transgressor to grow in their new mindset.

Waiting patiently for the healing of your spouse isn't as easy as it sounds. The transgressor needs to understand that an unhealed spouse is a hurt spouse. A hurt spouse will still say "ouch" from even a memory of the pain caused. They will be angry, stressed, emotionally sensitive, and even confused at times. This will be frustrating for the transgressor because, even after repentance is shown, they are being reminded of the damage they caused, even if it is in the past. This is rarely meant as a reminder or as a punitive "jab." This is the remnant of the wreckage. This is why patience is so essential. It's going to take time.

Step Two of Repair: Trust

Trust is developed through action. There must always be a demonstration of trustworthiness and trust-willingness for this pillar to be built or rebuilt. However, this step of repair is not about trust-building actions. It's about the commitment.

Each step has its own purpose. Empathy is all about taking action and is reinforced in safety. Together, empathy and safety simultaneously build trust through demonstration. But rebuilding broken trust takes commitment. Connections are pointless if someone refuses to trust again. Demonstration does not matter if one's character or integrity has not changed. So, rebuilding in this step will take commitment from both of you in order to achieve authentic repair.

To the Claimant

It's important to understand that, no matter how great or small the damage, repair cannot happen without you—even if it's not your fault, even if you have been completely blindsided by this emotional injury. Repairing your marriage depends on your participation in this process. Remember, being a claimant is not just about the damage; it's also about claiming the right to a benefit. In order to claim your benefit, you must show up.

The pillar of trust is a two-sided coin. Your side as the claimant is trust-willingness. This is the commitment to try to trust the transgressor again. This doesn't mean having blind faith or forcing yourself to forget what has been done. It means that you commit to acknowledging the transgressor's efforts.

What if they do it again?

What if they fail?

What if they just can't be right?

What if I get hurt again?

Feeling like this and having these fears are completely normal, but your commitment cannot be built on "what ifs." The fear of "what if" will paralyze you. It's not that these fears will magically disappear, but it's important that you do not allow the fear to keep you from moving forward.

Depending on the problem, or the level of hurt that has occurred, this may not be what you want to hear. After all, why should you have to do anything when you are the one that has been wronged? It's so easy to take this stance. And, in some instances, you'd be well within your right to feel this way. We don't want you to do anything that you're not ready to do or that you don't want to do. Many people struggle with the process of repair because they are crippled by the belief that repair means fixing things so your marriage goes back to being the way it was. In some cases, your marriage will never be the same again.

For many marriages, repair will mean finding a new place of origin and beginning. Yes, your new beginning can be fueled by your past and the feelings that led you to each other, but brokenness has changed you. So how you begin now will be different and will take more strength than when you first began. Even though being "as good as new" can happen for you, it will seem impossible from where you are standing right now. All we are asking is that you try and that you take this process step-by-step—one emotional, confused, and angry foot in front of the other.

To the Transgressor

The pillar of trust cannot be rebuilt without your commitment. In regards to the two-sided coin of the pillar, the side that you must commit to is trustworthiness. Your dilemma here is a little different. While the claimant's challenge is to trust someone outside of themselves, your challenge is to become worthy of their trust. This is a core adjustment.

At the place where trust was lost, there was a lack of integrity. This signifies a character issue for you. No matter the situation, your spouse has to be able to trust in who you are and who you promise them you are becoming. To be worthy of their trust requires a commitment to maturity and correction. It will take maturity to be able to step out of yourself and think about the impact of your choices. It will also take maturity to be able to receive correction in light of your choices.

Being committed to trustworthiness means that you will have to change. This is not just changing the behavior, which is easily accomplished through imitation. You must also commit to changing the why behind your behavior, also known as your motives. When catastrophe first hits a marriage, the very first thing a transgressor will do is make a 180-degree turn-around and imitate change in order to smooth things over in their marriage. They want to make their spouse feel better and get over their pain with the appearance of change. The reason why this never works is because the change is not genuine nor complete. Genuine change is when old self serving motives have changed to motives of serving the other.

As husbands and wives, our duty is in service to each other out of love. When trust has been broken, serving your spouse means demonstrating consistency and transparency in everything you do. Service to them after broken trust will mean considering them in your choices and making them aware of your choices on a consistent basis. It's being concerned with their wellbeing day to day, using empathy to feel where they are, and adjusting who you are for them. True service is always caring for them even when they don't see it, know it, or acknowledge it. It's committing to showing up for them, even when they don't always show up for you. It's sacrifice. When service is the motive, trustworthiness will be the outcome.

Depending on the level of hurt or damage that has been caused, it will seem like your efforts are pointless. Your spouse will seem cold at times, and they will be expecting you to give up when things don't turn around instantly. They will be waiting for you to disappoint them again, while at the same time begging inside for you to fight for their trust. The success of the repair process—and your marriage—depends on you to trust the process. You will not see the fruit of your efforts immediately. Just as you won't be able to change overnight, their feelings of hurt, rejection, or abandonment won't change overnight either. What will help them to change easier, and in some cases more rapidly, is your sincere commitment to change, growth, and earning their trust.

Step Three of Repair: Safety

When reviewing the steps of repair, empathy provided the connection and trust provided commitment. Rebuilding the pillar of safety is all about action. Safety, in the context of this chapter, will be all about creating an environment that gives both you and your spouse the necessary space and freedom needed to heal. You both must be physically safe in each other's presence. You both must be emotionally safe to feel and express your feelings without retaliation. You will both dictate the level of your spouse's safety by the environment you create for one another.

To the Transgressor

This is where your sincere apologies and genuine desire to change will meet your action. One of the most challenging parts about this process will be creating this environment of safety for your spouse, because it will not feel good. It will challenge you to rise to a level of selflessness that perhaps you haven't demonstrated in a long time. Allowing them to voice their hurt and frustrations, without becoming defensive;

serving them when it doesn't feel like they appreciate you; becoming accountable to them to ease their fears and anxiety; being open to their feelings without making them feel guilty for those feelings; and being transparent when you're used to thinking and acting autonomously is all about creating an environment of safety.

Your action in this process is not about erasing your mistake or simply "getting over" the pain that has been caused. Your spouse must see and feel that you are different than what you've already shown them. Wounds are easy to inflict, but they take time to heal. Your efforts towards making your spouse feel safe again will take time, consistency, and genuineness.

The Action

Reestablishing safety will revolve around what you do as well as who you are. To determine what to do, answer the following questions:

1. What was done that bothered, hurt, or broke your spouse?

2. How did that change your spouse's perception of you? *The answer to this will need to come from them.*

3. In what way does your spouse no longer feel safe with you? *Do they not feel safe to have a voice? Safe to be themselves? Safe from outside influences?*

4. Set aside some time to discuss what would make your spouse feel safe moving forward.
    a. Commit to hearing them and creating a habit of

making them feel safe by implementing their needs every day.

5. To the claimant: Your spouse will need to be safe with you too. It's important that you are helping to foster an environment of safety as well. Ask your spouse if there is anything that you can do to make them feel safer with you. *Perhaps by acknowledging their efforts? Minimizing hostility towards them? Ask them...then try. This is not about them defending their actions. This is only about you creating an environment of safety based on what is going on right now.*

Step Four of Repair: Security

Whenever we go to bed at night, Kenyon walks around the house and makes sure that all of the lights are out and doors are securely locked. That's what I depend on him to do. If one night he left the doors unlocked, and as a result we were robbed, it would be difficult for me to trust that he has done his job every night. I would constantly ask him, "Babe, did you lock the door? Are you sure?" And even though he will tell me yes, I might go and check for myself. I would be traumatized by the impact of that break-in, and it would take time for me to be able to trust that my husband has locked the door and that we are safe. This is what happens after a traumatic injury to your marriage.

Security is reestablished when your marriage has reached a place of normalcy again and the claimant has consistently observed the transgressor "locking the doors" to the marriage house through empathy, trust, and safety. Security is all about continuing the work that has been started. It's about continuing the new habits that you both began in rebuilding the pillar of safety, as well as growing beyond them. It's about seeking new ways to connect, showing your spouse how much you value and care for them, and spending time making them the first, front, and the center of your attention.

Under the pillar of security, you are vigilant and aware. Remember, opening the door to intimacy guarantees that there will be times that you will hurt one another, disagree, and have bad days. With continued vigilance of security, strengthened by the other pillars, our prayer is that you will navigate them without losing or removing your covering over each other ever again.

In Closing

As we were writing this book together, attempting to bring change to you, it changed us. It makes us proud to be able to say that this book, something that we wrote, became an incredible resource for us in our own marriage and blended family, enhancing our sensitivity and vigilance towards each other. We hope that this becomes an even more valuable resource for you and your family.

We were sincere when we said that we've found that the 4-Pillars are present in every single relationship. We pray that we've helped you to understand them and how vital to your

In Closing

marriage they are. For those who need further help, we are going to be conducting Marriage Accelerators, which will help couples go deeper in cultivating and recovering the 4-Pillars in their relationships. We'll hold them in private one- to three-day sessions with limited occupancy. To find out when a Marriage Accelerator will come to your state and which church or private location it'll be held at, visit us at CoveredMarriages.com.

Finally, there is one relationship that we have in which we are safe, where we are secure, and with whom we can trust that we are heard and understood. God knows what we need in our lives and in our marriages, even before we ask. He knows the sorrows of our hearts and the joys of our spirits. The Lord God is your safe haven. He is peace in the wars we fight. Our God and Father is the ultimate and unlimited covering.

God created you on purpose for relationship. He also created marriage on purpose to indulge in the deepest and most intimate relationship. Through your marriage, you are charged to be partners, ruling your part of this earth together. We pray that your marriage prospers in the endeavor of His will. We pray that you are healed where you need healing. We pray that you are strengthened where you need strength. We pray that God upholds you both, finishing this race together. We pray these things through the power of the cleansing blood of Jesus Christ. Amen.

www.ingramcontent.com/pod-product-compliance
Lightning Source LLC
Chambersburg PA
CBHW062022290426
44108CB00024B/2744